X

D0613808

GE

AR

Du

Through Lent with Luke

Daily Reflections on the Transfiguration and Passion

The Bible Reading Fellowship

- encourages regular, informed Bible-reading as a means of renewal in the churches

- issues various series of regular Bible readings with explanatory notes

- publishes introductory booklets on Bible-reading, group study guides, training aids, audio-visual material, etc.

Write or call now for full list of publications.

The Bible Reading Fellowship

St Michael's House	P.O. Box M	All Saints Parish
2 Elizabeth Street	Winter Park	P.O. Box 328
London SW1W 9RQ	Florida 32790	Dickson ACT 2602
	USA	Australia

MARGARET HEBBLETHWAITE

Through Lent with Luke

Daily Reflections
on the
Transfiguration and Passion

 the bible reading fellowship

6212

The Bible Reading Fellowship
St Michael's House
2 Elizabeth Street
London SW1W 9RQ

First Published 1986

Acknowledgements

The scripture quotations are from the Revised Standard Version © 1952, 1957 and 1971 by Division of Christian Education of the National Council of the Churches of Christ in the United States of America.

Pictures
(Front cover) Fernando Gallego (*fl.* 1466–1507), 'The Transfiguration': University of Arizona Museum of Art, gift of the Samuel H. Kress Foundation; photograph by Tim Fuller.

(Woodcuts) The publishers gratefully acknowledge help from the Warburg Institute (University of London), which supplied copyright prints as follows:
page 27 (Cornelis Massys, *c.* 1510–1570);
pages 43, 49, 59, 63, 65, 81, 95, 99, 104 (Albrecht Dürer, 1471–1528).

British Library CIP data

Hebblethwaite, Margaret
    Through Lent with Luke : daily reflections on the
    Transfiguration and Passion.
    1. Bible. N.T. Luke — Devotional literature
    I. Title II. Bible. N.T. Luke, *English*
    242'.2   BV85

    ISBN 0–900164–67–0

Printed by Bocardo & Church Army Press Ltd., Cowley, Oxford, England.

CONTENTS

FOREWORD

by Delia Smith

Margaret Hebblethwaite has 'caught' me in the very first paragraph of her book. I immediately found myself nodding in assent and identifying strongly with those who desperately try to fit in a last-minute meditation on the Passion into their busy schedule of Holy Week and preparing for Easter.

But now help is at hand. What she has carefully and skilfully set out for those whose lives are less ordered than they might be is a practical, helpful guide for meditation on the transfiguration and passion that starts at the very beginning of Lent. Thus her readers are invited to give a real commitment of measured time to ponder slowly and reflect on those events which led up to the death and resurrection of Jesus.

What I have found particularly helpful and inspiring is the fact that she has chosen to give us what she describes as Luke's 'especially beautiful and compassionate' account in concentrated form, taking the transfiguration and passion narratives verse by verse. It is only really possible to savour the richness of scripture if we take in very *little* at a time, allowing it through quiet reflection to penetrate and motivate us.

Margaret Hebblethwaite's own inspired reflections will nurture and guide us in our own meditation. What this book shows is how beautiful it can be to share another's intuition and insight, as food for reflection. If we are faithful to these daily meditations, the Risen Lord of Easter will accompany us on our journey, as he did on the road to Emmaus, and 'open our minds to understand the scriptures' (Luke 24:45).

INTRODUCTION

If you look at the cover of this book you will see Jesus in the moment of his transfiguration, holding out his hands in glory. Beneath him one of his disciples (probably John) holds up his own hands towards Jesus in wonder and welcome. Even John's face and garments reflect the brightness of the vision above him.

The transfiguration looks forward to the great glory of Easter, so it is a good place to begin a Lent book, which also looks forward to Easter. The events of those days will carry us through to the end of Lent, to the resurrection.

But if you look again at the cover-picture, you will notice something else. Those hands do not speak only of glory — they are also stretched out for the cross. Jesus opens his hands and John, in answer, lifts his hands upwards in a crucified gesture.

We may feel ourselves drawn into that gesture of John — offering ourselves freely with our eyes on Christ, to share his passion, to prepare for his glory. That is what this book is about — sharing the passion of Jesus, in our thoughts and prayers, to prepare ourselves for the Easter rising.

I have used Luke's gospel, partly because his version of the passion is especially beautiful and compassionate, partly because it is Luke that is used in the Roman Catholic liturgy for the year in which this book is published. I have followed his story steadily, a few verses at a time, through the two long sections surrounding the transfiguration and passion, just occasionally using a passage from a psalm or an epistle where it throws further light on the transfiguration. By taking a continuous narrative in very short steps we can go into depth on a little without losing sight of the whole.

Here and there through the book are engravings, mostly from Dürer's 'Little Passion' cycle. Sometimes a picture can lead us towards prayer better than words can, and stay longer in the memory.

. . . as he was praying.

Now it happened that as he was praying alone the disciples were with him.

(Luke 9:18)

Ash Wednesday is the first day of Lent. We have six-and-a-half weeks ahead of us, before we reach Easter. It is a great opportunity, a chance to spread out our thoughts about the passion, instead of trying to fit them all in the gaps between last-minute Easter preparations at the end of Holy Week. But it is quite a long time to keep up a resolution, even as simple a resolution as reading a Lent book. We need God's help and grace.

This book is divided up into daily readings, reflections and prayers. Every time we turn the page we enter a new day. Some readings are very short, like today's — just half a verse. But that is enough to feed a prayer. We have to learn to stop and listen, not to rush ahead.

Today's reading opens the section of Luke's gospel (Luke 9:18–45) that has the transfiguration at its heart, flanked by closely-knit events of prophecy and revelation. This section will take us through the first fortnight of Lent.

'As he was praying . . .' Prayer sets the tone for our daily reading, and embraces it from first to last. We know we should pray, because Jesus prayed. We follow his example. We ask him to be with us as we use this book, to be with us as we try to raise our hearts and minds towards him.

But we can look at it from the other side. It is not just a matter of Christ being with us as *we* pray, but, more profoundly, of us being with him as *he* prays. 'As he was praying alone the disciples were with him.' As Jesus prays we ask to be with him, to be drawn into his prayer. We do not just copy what he did, but rather unite ourselves to the praying Jesus so that he can pray in us. 'God has sent the Spirit of his Son into our hearts, crying, "Abba! Father!" ' (Galatians 4:6).

'As he was praying alone the disciples were with him.' Though the disciples were with him, Jesus was still alone. Prayer is always a time when we are alone. It is when we drop all our surrounding defences and distractions and gaze nakedly at the truth.

And yet prayer is also when we know quite decisively that we are not alone. When we pray God is with us, the praying Jesus is with us, the praying

Church is with us, throughout the world, throughout time, past and present, here and in the world to come. When we pray we enter into Jesus' aloneness. By becoming alone we realize that we are not alone.

As we begin this Lent prayerfully, we can become aware of the ways in which each of us feels alone. Perhaps we feel misunderstood. Perhaps we feel rejected. Perhaps we have suffered injustice. We all have some feelings along these lines.

Maybe we are afraid of unemployment . . . afraid of being abandoned by our children . . . by our spouse . . . by our friends . . . Maybe we are isolated by old age or by illness, or are stuck at home with a small baby.

Maybe it is death that we fear. Today, Ash Wednesday, is a day when we particularly remember that we must die, and return to the dust from which we came, naked and alone. That can be an uncomfortable thought.

These are feelings of loneliness. But prayer takes loneliness and turns it into graced aloneness. Loneliness is when we are alone and do not want to be alone. Prayer is when we choose to stand in that aloneness, because that is where we are with Christ.

Looking ahead we know how alone Jesus was to become. He was desperately alone as he suffered the torment of the cross, when his disciples betrayed him, denied him and fled. He had to be alone as he faced that beforehand in his prayer, preparing for the moment when no one could help him.

Today we choose to be with him in his aloneness.

Prayer May I be with you, Jesus,
in your prayer,
in your aloneness.

'. . . The Christ of God.'

. . . and he asked them, 'Who do the people say that I am?' And they answered, 'John the Baptist; but others say, Elijah; and others, that one of the old prophets has risen.' And he said to them, 'But who do you say that I am?' And Peter answered, 'The Christ of God.'

(Luke 9:18–20)

This profession of faith is a good place to start, because it reminds us of where we are: we are making these Lenten meditations for no other reason than because we do believe in Jesus. It is this act of faith that prepares us to set foot on the mountain along with Jesus — the mountain of transfiguration, and later on the mountain of Calvary.

When Jesus asks his disciples 'But who do you say that I am?', he must have known what a decisive question he was asking. If those closest to him did not give an answer of faith after all this time, then when would anyone realize he was the Christ? But it is important that he does not *tell* them — they must say it for themselves.

How can we imagine this exchange? A moment of quiet, following prayer. At first the easier question: who do *others* say that I am? And then the question that perhaps he had longed to ask but held back until now, just as we long to ask of someone we love: 'Do you love me?' and dare not in case we get the wrong answer. Jesus dares: 'But who do *you* say that I am?'

Was there a long silence before Peter was brave enough to speak for all of them? And if I had been there, would I have answered? Afterwards it is easy. Peter says 'The Christ of God,' Jesus confirms it, and now we can all join in with 'That's just what I would have said.' But would I? I think I would have kept silence, though I hope it would have been a silence of faith.

What do those four words mean anyway: 'the Christ of God'? The Greek word 'Christ', like the Hebrew word 'Messiah', means 'anointed'. The Christ is the 'anointed one' who was foretold to restore the rule of God in justice and peace. There are other ways of expressing this faith in Jesus. A little later on, on the mountain of transfiguration, the voice of God declares Jesus to be the Son of God, the Chosen One. When Jesus rides into Jerusalem the crowd greet him as 'the King who comes in the name of the Lord' (Luke 19:38). Son of God, Chosen One and King are all titles given in the Old Testament to the one who was to come to save us. And we might want to add the 'Word' of God, 'Lord', 'God incarnate', 'Second Person of the Trinity'.

So it was not only the title used by Peter that was important, but the way he said it and the fact that he said it. Of course that is not to say that it did not matter what he said — he needed to say rather more than 'one of the prophets'. But we can join in Peter's act of faith even without having exactly the same background of associations to 'the Christ' as he did.

We can imagine that after Peter had spoken, nothing would be the same again. It is like the moment when someone we love says 'I love you'. We may have suspected it, on both sides, even known it, in a sense. But once it is said, something new has happened. It is shared knowledge. It cannot be doubted. It cannot be unsaid. Jesus might have known that Peter knew, but would Peter have known that Jesus knew that he knew? And what about the other disciples who half-knew, and did not dare speak? Once it has been said, we can move forward with a sense of common understanding.

So it must have been for the disciples. Let it be so for us too. 'But who do you say that I am?' 'The Christ of God.' We, who were not there then, can be there now. We can make that act of faith our own.

Prayer I believe in you, Jesus.
        You are the Christ of God.

'. . . The Son of man must suffer.'

But he charged and commanded them to tell this to no one, saying, 'The Son of man must suffer many things, and be rejected by the elders and chief priests and scribes, and be killed, and on the third day be raised.'

(Luke 9:21–22)

Yesterday ended with a golden moment of recognition and shared knowledge, that Jesus is 'the Christ of God', but today's reading, that follows straight on without a break in Luke's gospel, adds a heavy weight to that happiness. No sooner do the disciples have it confirmed beyond doubt that Jesus is all they could possibly have hoped or suspected, than Jesus himself tells them with great seriousness, firstly that they must on no account share their happy knowledge with others, no matter how much they long to do so; but then, far worse, that he, the one they have all been waiting for from generation to generation, is about to be killed.

Little wonder that they did not want to hear this news, so that in Matthew and Mark's parallel accounts Peter takes Jesus aside and tells him to put the thought from him. We have a great capacity to disbelieve or ignore unwelcome warnings — particularly when they are warnings that we might lose someone we love. We close our eyes to the fact that our wife's smoking may cause her lung cancer, or that our husband has lost interest in us and comes home late every evening.

Here there was the added factor of genuine incomprehension. If Jesus was the Christ, then what he said about his rejection and suffering and death ran directly counter to everything they understood a Messiah to be. How could they accept what he said? How could they fail to look for an alternative explanation — that Jesus was speaking figuratively about spiritual sufferings, perhaps, or that quite simply Jesus had made a mistake, and this was a minor part of his teaching that could be ignored.

It is all very well for us to laugh at the obtuseness of the disciples, but we only came to hear about Jesus at all after he had died and risen. And even so, many of us know quite well what trouble we have in accepting that Jesus is a Messiah of this kind. Do we really want a Saviour who dies on a cross for us, with all the guilt that comes when we compare that mortifying generosity

14

with our own mistrust and selfishness? Would we not so much rather an unspoilt blaze of triumph and happiness for our King and Lord, so that we could ride at his side proudly, without a sense of inadequacy and fear?

Jesus knew all these techniques for avoiding the truth, and prophesies his passion quite clearly both now, and just after his transfiguration. And in Matthew and Mark's accounts he needs to rebuke Peter quite savagely for the temptation he had laid before him. 'Get behind me, Satan! For you are not on the side of God, but of men.'

But the gloom of this prophecy is found in our own fearful hearts, not in the facts themselves. To save us is an act of glory. To be raised on the third day (as the prophecy ends) is an act of glory. The glory is all the greater for the suffering and failure that will precede it and that will be routed.

How the disciples must have longed to enjoy the presence of their newly acknowledged Christ, without this death sentence over-shadowing the joy of their hearts! And yet Jesus knew how important it was to prepare them, way in advance. If he had not done so, then the disciples would have had good cause to see his death as a failure. As it was, the repeated though ignored warnings at least gave the possibility that in the time of apparently total despair they could remember, and wait for the third day.

It did not seem that many, if any, of the disciples found themselves able to respond like that when his death came. Certainly the stories that survive are of unbelief: 'O foolish men, and slow of heart to believe all that the prophets have spoken! Was it not necessary that the Christ should suffer these things and enter into his glory?' (Luke 24:25–26). But in today's gloomy warning, in the unwelcome shadow over the joyful knowledge of who Jesus was, at least he gave them a chance.

Prayer Help me hear the unwelcome warnings of my own life.
Show me how to face up to those things I most fear.
Bring me into the greater glory on the other side of pain, and rejection, and death.

'. . . take up his cross daily.'

And he said to all, 'If any man would come after me, let him deny himself and take up his cross daily and follow me. For whoever would save his life will lose it; and whoever loses his life for my sake, he will save it. For what does it profit a man if he gains the whole world and loses or forfeits himself? For whoever is ashamed of me and of my words, of him will the Son of man be ashamed when he comes in his glory and the glory of the Father and of the holy angels. But I tell you truly, there are some standing here who will not taste death before they see the kingdom of God.'

(Luke 9:23–27)

Yesterday we touched on the truth that having a Saviour who suffers, and is rejected, and dies for our sakes, confronts us with the unwelcome knowledge that we are too cowardly to take such a path ourselves. And today that truth is rubbed in, as Jesus announces quite bluntly that anyone who wants to follow him must take up his cross, daily. It is not something we rejoice to hear, unless we trivialize it in a self-justifying fashion and say, 'Waiting in that traffic jam this morning was my cross. Listening to that tedious man at the office yesterday was my cross.' In such a way we can end up reassuring ourselves that nothing in our lives needs altering, whereas what Jesus means to do here is rather to jolt us into realizing how far we fall short.

It is easy to be depressed by this text. It may be not so much the idea of losing our lives that is alarming, nor the demand to have no shame in Christ, but rather the need to carry the cross daily. Crosses are heavy. How can we not feel heavy within ourselves at the prospect?

We may be helped if we remember that all those who followed Jesus did so without weighing up the consequences first. The disciples instantly obeyed Jesus' call to follow him. 'Come, follow me,' Jesus would say, and straightaway without a moment of consideration or soul-searching, each apostle rose and went. There is line of a hymn that goes: 'Let us like them, without a word, rise up and follow thee'.

The truth is that there is just no question about it. Once we have known Christ and believed in him, there is no second thought possible. Jesus may warn us of dreadful prospects on the path ahead, and we can just laugh at them. There can be no question of doing anything else but following Christ. Burdens and pains are nothing in comparison with the clarity of our knowledge that what we must do is follow.

It is like the story Jesus told about the man who found a treasure in a field and sold all he had to buy that field. He did not do this with any reluctance — not even when he lost every single thing he had possessed. No, he did it 'in joy', he had no doubt about it. He was so clear in his own mind that what he wanted to do was to own that field, that he did not even notice the pain of losing everything else in the process.

We may be able to remember moments in our life when something joyful took from us any sense of heaviness at the sacrifices that were asked. We might, for example, remember how happily we moved into cheap digs instead of staying in the comfort of our parents' home, for the joy of being free and adult. Or we might remember the happiness of sharing all our worldly possessions with the man or woman we wanted to marry. Or we might remember how the joy of a first child made us quite forget about the work and exhaustion of looking after a baby.

And so, 'in joy' let us declare ourselves willing to take up our cross — that light yoke and that sweet burden — and to lose all that we have for the sake of Christ, even our lives. And then we can stand in the glory of God when the Son of man comes to welcome us.

Prayer   I want to follow you, Jesus,
         even carrying my cross.

... about eight days after.

Now about eight days after these sayings he took with him Peter and John and James, and went up on the mountain to pray. And as he was praying, the appearance of his countenance was altered, and his raiment became dazzling white. And behold, two men talked with him, Moses and Elijah, who appeared in glory and spoke of his departure, which he was to accomplish at Jerusalem. Now Peter and those who were with him were heavy with sleep, and when they wakened they saw his glory and the two men who stood with him. And as the men were parting from him, Peter said to Jesus, 'Master, it is well that we are here; let us make three booths, one for you and one for Moses and one for Elijah' — not knowing what he said. As he said this, a cloud came and overshadowed them; and they were afraid as they entered the cloud. And a voice came out of the cloud, saying, 'This is my Son, my Chosen; listen to him!' And when the voice had spoken, Jesus was found alone. And they kept silence and told no one in those days anything of what they had seen.

(Luke 9:28–36)

Every Sunday, even in Lent, is a little feast-day of the glory of the resurrection; so this First Sunday of Lent is a good moment for looking over the transfiguration story, taken as a whole, before splitting it up into shorter passages for meditation during the week ahead. We shall spend all this week on the mystery of the transfiguration.

The most obvious way in which the transfiguration looks ahead is in the glory that was revealed there: for a brief space, Jesus steps ahead into the glory of the resurrection. But, less obviously, the transfiguration also looks forward to the passion, and this is marked by several narrative parallels between the two stories.

First of all, we can mention the theme of the mountain. Jesus climbs a mountain for the transfiguration, just as later he was to climb the Mount of Olives for his arrest and the hill of Calvary for his death.

Secondly, it is interesting that the three disciples chosen to climb the mountain of the transfiguration — Peter, John and James — are the same three who in Matthew and Mark's accounts are asked to go forward with

Jesus in Gethsemane to watch with him. And, as in Gethsemane, they are heavy with sleep.

These three onlookers — Peter, James and John — are confronted by three figures — Moses and Elijah, with Jesus at the centre. Similarly, on Calvary, Jesus is at the centre of a threesome, and the three crosses there complement Peter's idea of three booths at the transfiguration.

The talk between Jesus, Moses and Elijah, also looks ahead to the passion, because they talk about Jesus' 'departure, which he was to accomplish at Jerusalem' (9:31). There is no contradiction between the glory of the transfiguration, and the pain of the passion. On the contrary, it is only as Jesus faces the suffering that is to come — talking about it, first to the disciples, and now to the prophets — that he enters his state of transfiguration.

One final pre-figuring of the passion can be mentioned. When Jesus was on the cross, 'there was darkness over the whole land until the ninth hour' (Luke 23:44). Here, at the transfiguration, a similar darkness descends: 'a cloud came and overshadowed them; and they were afraid as they entered the cloud' (9:34). It seems that both crucifixion and transfiguration present sights too awesome for human eyes to bear. The supreme reality presented in the events is blinding to our vision. There can be no glory without the cloud of darkness and of fear.

Prayer There have been moments of light in my life,
        moments of deep faith,
        moments of unsuspected joy,
        moments of burning love.
        I remember them before you, my God.

. . . on the mountain.

Now about eight days after these sayings he took with him Peter and John and James, and went up on the mountain to pray. And as he was praying, the appearance of his countenance was altered, and his raiment became dazzling white. And behold, two men talked with him, Moses and Elijah, who appeared in glory and spoke of his departure, which he was to accomplish at Jerusalem.

(Luke 9:28–31)

Again these verses appear in our daily reading, but they are so rich that we can dwell on them again and again, each time taking a shorter passage. Over the next few days we will continue through the transfiguration story, a few verses at a time.

We have already seen how Jesus, who was betrayed on a mount, and crucified on another mount, now climbs a mountain to pray. Mountains were very important in Jesus' life and ministry, and figured on other occasions as well. Jesus was tempted on a mountain in the wilderness, when the devil showed him all the kingdoms of the world (Matthew 4:8–9). Much of Jesus' most important teaching is put in the setting of the Sermon on the Mount (Matthew 5:1ff). Jesus' triumphal entry into Jerusalem begins from another mount — Mount Olivet, or the Mount of Olives (Luke 19:29, 37). Finally, he ascended into heaven from the same Mount Olivet (Acts 1:12).

It is not difficult to understand why mountains should have been chosen as the settings for these most precious moments in Jesus' life and death. Mountains reach towards the skies; mountains require effort to climb, and deter the lazy and half-hearted; mountains are places of barren beauty and pure air. It is not hard to think of them as places where a decisive encounter with God can be made.

Mountains are dangerous places too. They have cliffs and precipices. They are often swept up in clouds and mists that can threaten the life of anyone without a compass. Mountains are often cold, and there is no wind like the wind on the top of a mountain. But from a mountain, one can see with such clarity and so far . . . and the world looks so full of beauty. And so we feel that from a mountain we see things a little bit more with God's eyes.

It is only a symbol, of course, but a good one. And along with the privileged view, goes the risk and the discomfort — the sense that if human beings want to stray into God's territory, then they may face more than they bargained for. They must take risks; they must climb slowly and with patience; they must ache from the effort; they must lose their lives if they become over-bold.

So Jesus, when he wanted to pray, went up a mountain. Where else?

'And as he was praying, the appearance of his countenance was altered, and his raiment became dazzling white.' We are not told in Luke how his face was altered — the Greek just says it was 'other', though Matthew says it 'shone like the sun'. We may be reminded how the face of the risen Christ was often 'other', so that his closest friends did not recognize him.

A literal translation of the second half of that sentence would be 'his clothes flashed like white lightning'. But we are not just confronted with a naturally beautiful moment, as when the sun shines brightly on a white garment. There may have been that as well, of course, but there is more: there is the bodily presence of two saintly men from past history, seen and heard not only by Jesus, in his mystical moment, but by the disciples who stayed outside the event and yet are able to observe everything. What is happening is a manifestation of glory — a glory that envelops Moses and Elijah as well as Jesus, but that must be, in the end, the glory of God. We remember John's words at the end of his Prologue: 'we have beheld his glory, glory as of the only Son from the Father' (John 1:14).

Prayer   May I behold your glory,
           glory as of the only Son from the Father.

. . . they saw his glory.

Now Peter and those who were with him were heavy with sleep, and when they wakened they saw his glory and the two men who stood with him. And as the men were parting from him, Peter said to Jesus, 'Master, it is well that we are here; let us make three booths, one for you and one for Moses and one for Elijah' — not knowing what he said.

(Luke 9:32–33)

In these verses our attention shifts from Jesus and the two prophets, to Peter, James and John as they observed the events. They 'were heavy with sleep, and when they wakened they saw this glory'. This time they do not wake to the shame of their own weakness — as they were to do in Gethsemane. They awake to the vision of glory, rather as we hope to do when we fall into the sleep of death, and awake to see God's face.

Notice that there is no suggestion that they were dreaming, although that would have been the most obvious 'explanation' of their experience. No, they woke, not to illusion, but to a greater reality. They saw the truth, and could not doubt it, even though months passed with their lips sealed in silence, when they might have been tempted to doubt their secret memories.

'They saw his glory.' It is no longer just a matter of having faith in Jesus as 'the Christ of God', but they glimpse with their own eyes the glory that was his before the world was made (John 17:5) and that would be his again after he had suffered and so entered into his glory (Luke 24:26).

When Moses asked to see the glory of God on Mount Sinai he was hidden in a cleft of the rock with his face covered while the glory of God passed by, for no one can see God and live (Exodus 33:20). He came down from speaking with God and the skin of his face shone so that people were afraid to come near him (Exodus 34:30). So, when Peter, James and John wake to see the glory of Christ they find themselves on the edge of the life beyond, rather like children who wake late in the evening to overhear conversations that were not intended for their ears, that they cannot understand, and that they may find disturbing. The vision of glory is not normally intended for us in this life, and Peter, James and John cannot tell others what they have seen when they come down the mountain.

They see 'the two men who stood with him', Moses and Elijah. These were among the very greatest heroes of their upbringing, and had they seen no more than that they would already have had a quite extraordinary vision. But the two men are caught up in the light of Christ, and the three disciples see the man they have loved and followed shining with the glory that is really his, but that has been hidden from their sight.

It was the kind of experience of which we use the old, clichéd phrase: 'he rubbed his eyes'. Peter did not know what to say. He felt he was in the presence of an event so sacred that it must be commemorated. The booths that he proposed were reminiscent of the tabernacle in the wilderness that was built to enshrine the sacred presence of God. It was the Jewish equivalent of building three shrines or chapels on the mountain-top.

We may wonder why Luke seemed to regard it as such a stupid suggestion. Was it the impracticality of the scheme — for they had no materials with them, and even if they were to bring them, a tent or booth would not last long without someone to attend to it? Or was it that they had so entered the age of the kingdom, in which God is worshipped 'neither on this mountain nor in Jerusalem . . . but in spirit and truth' (John 4:21, 24), that the whole idea of commemorative shrines was a thing outgrown? Or was it just the wrong moment to think of it?

Whatever the reason, Peter was once again acting as spokesman for the others, and this time voicing, in his own brave and somewhat clumsy way, the recognition that here was a truth so precious, so beautiful and so awesome, that what they wanted to do was to fall down and worship.

One day we will each wake from the sleep of death to see God's glory, and to find again those we love and admire, shining in that glory. However much, like Peter, we already have faith, it cannot help but come as a surprise. And then, as Moses and Elijah did, we too will speak with Jesus face to face.

Prayer Prepare me to wake into the vision of your glory,
  so that I may be overcome with humility, but not shame;
  with adoration, but not embarrassment.

. . . a cloud came.

As he said this, a cloud came and overshadowed them; and they were afraid as they entered the cloud.

(Luke 9:34)

How wonderful it would be if all we had to do was to fall asleep, and then wake up into the glory of God! But it is not as simple as that. After only a brief spell of dwelling in the glorious light of the transfigured Christ with the saints of heaven, Peter and his companions are plunged into darkness and even fear. A cloud comes down and overshadows them — they can no longer see — and they are afraid as they enter the cloud.

Entering a cloud is a form of poverty. It means giving up our sight and our vision ahead. It means not knowing where we are or how long it will be before we can see again. And that is frightening because it means entering the unknown.

We can recall what we were saying earlier about the danger of mountains, where mist can suddenly descend and make climbers lose their way. Were it no more than a purely natural descent of thick cloud on the apostles, there might already have been some cause for alarm. But this mist is far more than that. It brings the fear of God. It is the cloud of unknowing. It is the dark night of the soul.

We all must enter this dark cloud in one way or another. The author of the medieval anonymous work, the *Cloud of Unknowing*, said this:

'This cloud and this darkness, no matter what you do, is between you and your God. It prevents you from seeing him clearly with your mind and from experiencing the sweetness of his love in your heart. Prepare yourself to wait in this darkness as long as you may, ever calling after him whom you love. If ever you shall feel him or see him — as far as is possible here below — it must always be in this cloud and this darkness' (*Cloud of Unknowing*, chapter 3).

'If ever you shall see him — as far as is possible here below . . . ' The disciples had almost stepped beyond that, almost stood in the heavenly places, but it was too early. They were not yet dead and buried and risen with Christ. They may have been on a mountain-top, half way to heaven, they may have glimpsed . . . but then the earthly situation overshadows them again. They are still in the 'here below'. They still must wait and trust and be enveloped in the cloud of unseeing. The promise is not for yet.

We all know the feeling of darkness between ourselves and God. We feel the frustration and bewilderment of not seeing God clearly with our mind and of not experiencing the sweetness we long for — the sweetness of his love in our heart. But we make a mistake if we think this cloud is a failure. What God wants us to do is to call after him, and we often call loudest and most persistently for God when we are in the cloud, feeling frightened and lost.

So long as in our cloud we are calling after him whom we love, then we are not failing but succeeding. The sweetness and the light will come with great certainty if we have learnt to call after him in our heart, and he will be a greater sweetness and a more blinding light the more we have learnt to long for him.

Often we feel guilty about our depressions and desolations, as though they were our fault, and if only we had learnt to think about the situation in the right way then we would no longer feel distressed. But our faith reassures us that is not so. We must go through the dark patches, and we cannot hurry them. We are not called to pull ourselves together, or shake ourselves out of it, but to find our way of relating to God from where we are. It will not, for the moment, be the full, sweet vision of his felt presence, but it may be something more valuable than that — a learning of dependence, weakness and need, that can form the only firm foundation for our relationship with God.

Prayer Give me strength to wait in the darkness,
        learning to call after you.

'... my Son, my Chosen.'

And a voice came out of the cloud, saying, 'This is my Son, my Chosen; listen to him!'

(Luke 9:35)

Here is a triumphant confirmation from heaven of Peter's act of faith. Peter has declared Jesus 'the Christ of God'. Now the voice from the cloud proclaims him indeed to be of God, to be God's Son; it proclaims him indeed to be the anointed Christ-Messiah, for he is the Chosen One. If we put these titles — 'Christ of God', 'Son of God', 'Chosen of God' — in the simplest possible form for us today, we could just say that this is the man in whom we must have faith. And because he is the man in whom we must have faith, he is the man to whom we must listen.

'Listen to him!' Very soon, when they come down from the mountain, Jesus will prophesy his passion for the second time. And will the disciples listen? Will they heed the voice from heaven, to listen and believe the words of the Son of God?

That challenge is very shortly ahead. But for the moment we are left with the picture of Jesus Christ, his arms stretched out, presented to us in power. 'This is my Son.' He had stretched out his arms to pray, in the traditional gesture of prayer that can be observed in many paintings from the catacombs and sculptures from early sarcophagi. He had stretched out his arms in anticipation of the crucifixion of which he was speaking to Moses and Elijah. He stretched out his arms in welcome, in self-giving and vulnerability. He stretched out his arms to open up the way to his heart, and to embrace us all. And again, he stretched out his arms in glory and triumph, as a runner breaks the tape or a politician acknowledges his victory. He stretched out his arms in the glory of God to which he will soon ascend, when he is seated at the right hand of the Father. In prayer, in sacrifice, in glory, Jesus gives himself to us with his arms outstretched. And God, too, gives him to us: 'This is my Son, my Chosen'.

Prayer You stretch out your arms for me,
        and I stretch out my arms to receive you,
        Jesus, Son of God, Chosen One.

... fire goes before him.

The LORD reigns; let the earth rejoice;
  let the many coastlands be glad!
Clouds and thick darkness are round about him;
  righteousness and justice are the foundation of his throne.
Fire goes before him,
  and burns up his adversaries round about.
His lightnings lighten the world;
  the earth sees and trembles.
The mountains melt like wax before the LORD,
  before the Lord of all the earth.
The heavens proclaim his righteousness;
  and all the peoples behold his glory.

(Psalm 97:1–6)

This psalm comes from the Roman Catholic lectionary for the feast of the transfiguration. And the very day on which I am writing this (though not the day on which you are reading it) is by chance the feast of the transfiguration. This very day, the feast of the transfiguration, is also the anniversary of the bombing of Hiroshima. Hiroshima and the transfiguration have become eternally bound together, as the sin of humanity horrifically apes the judgment of God. What better way of uniting Hiroshima with the transfiguration, than by seeing both in the light of the passion, which alone gives meaning to both events?

'The LORD reigns; let the earth rejoice.' Let it be the Lord alone who reigns, for it is the worst form of blasphemy and idolatry for human beings to take upon themselves the authority of God. I do not wish to make a judgment upon what the United States ought to have done when faced with the war with Japan, or whether it would have been better to have fought a long and weary and bloody campaign, draining out the blood drop by drop instead of drawing a quick end by a sudden holocaust. Nor do I pretend to know who ought to have done what, and when. I simply say that a world in which people drop nuclear bombs on each other is a hopeless mess of sin. If the Lord reigns, let the earth indeed rejoice, but when sinful man reigns, let the earth mourn.

'Clouds and thick darkness are round about him.' Let the cloud not be the mushroom cloud, nor the darkness the nuclear winter threatened by the dust-clouds of large-scale nuclear attack. Let these not be, for the foundation we seek is the 'righteousness and justice' of God, not war between man and man.

'Fire goes before him, and burns up his adversaries round about.' Can it be true, that the Hiroshima disaster has mimicked so grotesquely every word of this psalm? When man plays at God, then we recoil in horror.

'His lightnings lighten the world; the earth sees and trembles.' And so did the bright flash of Hiroshima, that made the faces of those who gazed at it peel off, leaving them disfigured. We see and tremble.

'The mountains melt like wax before the LORD, before the Lord of all the earth.' The furnace of the nuclear explosion could aptly be described as melting mountains like wax. But if the mountains are to melt, please God it may be before the glory of the Lord, not before the blasphemous blast of nuclear destruction.

'The heavens proclaim his righteousness; and all the peoples behold his glory.' So be it. May we behold his glory, and his righteousness, and if that burns us up, shrivels us to dust, melts us and changes us, then may we welcome it, for that burning — before the great glory of God — is not carnage but conversion.

And those who have died, in the horror and the unrighteousness, have beauty now, for they are united with the Christ who, contemplating the horror and unrighteousness of his coming death, was transfigured in the glory that he was soon to enjoy for ever. The innocents who died must now be in the land of rejoicing and gladness. But we sinful beings who remain, and who are implicated, however distantly, in the sin of playing at being God, we are the ones who need to tremble.

Prayer May we behold your glory, Lord,
and may no other fire burn us up, but your fire.

. . . we were with him on the holy mountain.

For we did not follow cleverly devised myths when we made known to you the power and coming of our Lord Jesus Christ, but we were eye-witnesses of his majesty. For when he received honour and glory from God the Father and the voice was borne to him by the Majestic Glory, 'This is my beloved Son, with whom I am well pleased,' we heard this voice borne from heaven, for we were with him on the holy mountain. And we have the prophetic word made more sure. You will do well to pay attention to this as to a lamp shining in a dark place, until the day dawns and the morning star rises in your hearts.

(2 Peter 1:16–19)

This wonderful account of the transfiguration comes not in a gospel, but in the second epistle of Peter. Like the psalm we used yesterday, this is one of the readings for the feast of the transfiguration. The author (whom some scholars think was not in fact Peter the apostle) speaks as though he was a first-hand eye-witness, 'for we were with him on the holy mountain'. It is moving, after all these days in which we have been meditating on the transfiguration, to turn the page and find ourselves confronted with the vividness of those words. We, who read the letter, almost feel taken up with Peter onto that holy mountain and into that glorious presence.

If there is a special emphasis to this apparently eye-witness account, it is on glory. Glory even appears as a name, given a capital letter in the RSV translation, to refer to God — the 'Majestic Glory'. And similar words abound: 'power', 'majesty', 'honour', 'glory'. The prayer that we make to God the Father — 'For thine is the kingdom, the power and the glory' — is turned round by God and reflected straight onto his Son Jesus. So great is the glory of Christ on the mountain that Peter even speaks as though what happened was not just a revelation of an existing glory, nor even a looking ahead to a future glory, but an actual moment of conferring glory on Christ: 'for when he received honour and glory from God . . . we were with him.'

They were with him, and they saw, and they heard. Any spiritualizing interpretation is pushed aside by the writer — he lays all the stress on actual sense experience. We find this hard to take. Even if we are prepared to believe that there was a historic event on a mountain, and that there was something to see — a glow in the sun, an inner radiance — we baulk at the suggestion that there was an audible voice. A voice in the heart, maybe. But words borne from the sky?

The words spoken are similar to Luke's version — 'This is my Son, my Chosen,' — but identical to Matthew's account — 'This is my beloved Son, with whom I am well pleased.' They are also identical to the words spoken at Jesus' baptism in Matthew, while in Mark and Luke the words at the baptism are addressed to Jesus himself: 'Thou art my beloved Son; with thee I am well pleased' (Luke 3:22).

If the transfiguration is a reminder and confirmation of the baptismal revelation, it is also a forward pointer. For the author of the epistle it is a pledge, not only of the glory of resurrection and ascension, but of the second coming. The word used for 'coming' at the beginning of the passage is '*parousia*' — a word often used for the second coming of Christ — and at the end of the passage the phrase 'until the day dawns' also makes us look ahead to the future coming.

And so Peter, who has once glimpsed, and once heard the voice borne from heaven, keeps these memories in his heart like 'a lamp shining in a dark place' — a lamp that, for all its brightness, will one day be dwarfed by the full blaze of the new dawn.

Prayer May your transfiguration be a lamp to me,
                until the day dawns,
                and the morning star rises in my heart.

. . . they kept silence.

And when the voice had spoken, Jesus was found alone. And they kept silence and told no one in those days anything of what they had seen.

(Luke 9:36)

On the First Sunday of Lent we began to meditate on the transfiguration. This Sunday, we draw that mystery to a close, while over the next few days we shall look at the events immediately following the transfiguration.

There is something wonderfully undramatic about this last verse of the story. We have been exalted to enormous heights, dragged through exaltation and self-offering, through supernatural visions and auditions, through exhilaration and fear. Now the prophets have gone, the voice ceases, the cloud passes . . . and all is as it was, all is normal. Jesus is found alone. And the disciples do not even speak about the extraordinary experience they have been through.

I said there is something wonderful about this lack of drama. After an enormous emotional drain — however thrilling — there is a security in going back to ordinary life. We love to have adventures and to feel we have been favoured with special experiences, but we do not want to live at that pitch of fervour all the time. The return to normality is like the comfort of a warm and familiar bed at the end of a full and exhausting day.

All is as it was. And yet something has changed. Even if the disciples must keep their experiences secret, they have still seen something they could not have imagined, and heard something they could not have invented. What has changed is within themselves, as we saw yesterday — their own faith in Jesus; their own hope in the glory to come; their consequent love for others who, without their privileged vision, are yet heirs to that glory. Everything is normal and familiar once more, and yet the vision has power to change it all, if they will but remember it, if they will but listen to the Son of God.

The transfiguration is a tremendous mystery, because it is a pledge of the future, and we, now, need that just as much as Peter, James and John — indeed Jesus himself— needed it then. We need to know that no matter what we go through, no matter how pointless, and unjust, and lunatic it all seems, no matter how much the world collapses around us, that glory is there waiting for us.

The tremendous comfort of that glory is that it is not *our* glory — it does not depend on us at all — it is God's glory, and depends on him. But we can share in it, as Moses and Elijah shared in it. We can be transformed, and radiant with it, if we submit to God's majesty; and that includes submitting to our death, as Jesus submitted to his death.

The great pledge of the transfiguration takes us through dryness and through pain, through boredom and through fear, through living and through dying. We can be perfectly at ease in the ordinariness of everyday life, because we have a pledge of what is inside and beyond it. And we can thank God that, with that pledge, we do not have to go through the exhaustion of seeing everything in full reality all the time. As we put on dark glasses against the glare of the sun, so God protects us against the constant vision of the transfiguration, not so that we should doubt it, but so that we should get on with working for his kingdom while we are not prostrate with awe and fear before his power and glory.

Prayer I keep silence before you, Lord.
          Not a silence of forgetting,
          but a silence of remembering your glory.

'. . . a spirit seizes him.'

On the next day, when they had come down from the mountain, a great crowd met him. And behold, a man from the crowd cried, 'Teacher, I beg you to look upon my son, for he is my only child; and behold, a spirit seizes him, and he suddenly cries out; it convulses him till he foams, and shatters him, and will hardly leave him. And I begged your disciples to cast it out, but they could not.'

(Luke 9:37–40)

After what was probably the most intense religious experience of their lives so far, Peter, James, John and Jesus come down from the mountain. It is not clear how long they had stayed on the mountain top, though at least one night was included.

Perhaps the transfiguration happened in the full blaze of the afternoon sun, while the disciples were taking a siesta after their morning's climb. Then they would have lived out an evening and a night in the shadow of their experience, and made a fresh day's start on their return journey. But I prefer to think the transfiguration, like the resurrection, occurred at dawn, after Jesus had, in characteristic style, spent a night in prayer (he does this in Luke 6:12). This would explain why the disciples had been heavy with sleep. And in this case their return 'the next day' might mean 'the coming day', the day following the dawn events.

Whichever way it was, they must have descended the mountain with an extraordinary mixture of emotions — stimulation, and emotional draining, the thrill of seeing the glory of God, reluctance to leave it, relief to get back to the solid earth of the plains, sheer tiredness, and a sense of unreality and distance as they plunge again into a world of people who have not seen as they have seen.

Probably the last thing they felt like facing was the scene that actually met them. One scripture scholar, Alfred Plummer, spoke of it like this: 'the chosen three blinded by the light, the remaining nine baffled by the powers of darkness'. The contrast could not be more dramatic between the good, clear, blinding light of God's glory above, and the evil, confused, destructive powers of darkness here below. Coming from the realms of their glimpse of the heavens, they find themselves in the thick of panic, pain and fear, as the distraught father begs and pleads for help, and the poor disciples struggle against a power of evil too strong for them to control.

And so, when Jesus arrives — this Jesus who had left them alone, to face a devil that they could not conquer — how they must have rushed to him with relief — disciples, and father, and 'great crowd' along with them. Here at last was their help and healing, and the father cries out, pouring out his pain before the Lord. 'Teacher, I beg you . . . for he is my only child . . . a spirit seizes him . . . it convulses him till he foams, and shatters him, and will hardly leave him.' It is a poignant tale of fear, from a man who turns to Jesus with deep entreaty, because he has no one else to whom he may turn. For 'I begged your disciples to cast it out, but they could not.'

And so the Son of God, barely returned from the glory of the mountain, already looking ahead to the powers of evil he must meet in his passion, now finds himself faced by the chaos and damage that a single unclean spirit can bring.

Prayer I, too, come to meet you, Jesus,
           bringing the sin and confusion within me,
           for you to heal.

'. . . how long am I to be with you?'

Jesus answered, 'O faithless and perverse generation, how long am I to be with you and bear with you? Bring your son here.' While he was coming, the demon tore him and convulsed him. But Jesus rebuked the unclean spirit, and healed the boy, and gave him back to his father. And all were astonished at the majesty of God.

(Luke 9:41–43)

The father's poignant plea for help draws from Jesus an amazingly severe reproach. It is probably not directed at him — in fact it is rather difficult to see quite who it is directed against. Perhaps against his own apostles, whose faith was insufficient to heal the boy? Perhaps against the relations and friends of the boy, whose faith was likewise inadequate? Perhaps against the crowd in general, who for some reason we cannot quite fathom had angered Jesus? 'O faithless and perverse generation, how long am I to be with you and bear with you?' They are strong words, beyond what we might have thought was justified, certainly beyond what the apostles might have thought justified, left as they had been to cope with a situation they could not handle.

We can only guess at what these strong words mean, and they may mean something different to each of us. Sometimes it is the most difficult words of scripture that can end up yielding surprising fruit. But here are some avenues of approach; one or other of them may help.

We can imagine how disturbing it would be if anyone — friend or enemy — turned on us and said, 'You are faithless and perverse. How long have I got to put up with you?' If Jesus said it — from whom we long to hear words of approval and reassurance — how much more upsetting it would be! So our first lesson from these words might be to be shaken out of complacency. He who had the patience to say 'Father, forgive them; for they know not what they do,' also had the impatience to cut short any needless hesitancy and sweep angrily aside those who stood in the way and vacillated. It is as though Jesus is saying, 'Let's cut through the nonsense and get on with it'.

It may be that Jesus felt his disciples showed excessive dependence on him. If they had only had enough faith they could perfectly well have driven out the devil, instead of rushing to him like helpless children who get into a panic as soon as their mother has gone out of the room. It is irritating when people pretend they cannot manage without us, as a ploy to keep us with them.

There may have been another strand in Jesus' response. Coming, as he did, from a marvellous mystical experience, and being confronted not only by the continual wearing presence of evil but also by the incapacity of people to pull themselves out of sinful situations, he may even have looked forward to his death. 'How long am I to be with you and bear with you?' That exodus, that departure, that he had prayed over and talked over and been mystically caught up into on the mountain-top, stayed with him and called him to itself, so he longed to be free of this constricting world. He longed to end it all — all the wearisome day-to-day chipping away at sin and pain here and there, bit by bit, while ever more mountains of needy people flocked to him for his help. His death would overcome the powers of sin once and for all. 'I came to cast fire upon the earth; and would that it were already kindled! I have a baptism to be baptized with; and how I am constrained until it is accomplished!' (Luke 12:49–50)

But these words of impatience are no more than the prelude to an act of mercy and love. Jesus wastes no time in calling the boy to him. The devil puts up a last desperate fight; but quickly Jesus commands him to depart and the boy is healed. While Mark spins out this story, in his parallel text, into a great battle between Christ and Satan, Luke presents it in far simpler terms. Once Jesus had rebuked the evil spirit there is no more to be said — the battle is over.

'And all were astonished at the majesty of God.' That majesty that was manifested on the mountain, through the transfiguration, is here below manifested in a different, but just as powerful a form. The power of God is not just beauty and radiance, but also healing and mercy. It is not self-contained and inward-looking: it reaches out to transform the world.

Prayer Teach me to stand on my own feet.
Teach me to be decisive, and to have faith in you.

. . . they were afraid to ask.

But while they were all marvelling at everything he did, he said to his disciples, 'Let these words sink into your ears; for the Son of man is to be delivered into the hands of men.' But they did not understand this saying, and it was concealed from them, that they should not perceive it; and they were afraid to ask him about this saying.

(Luke 9:43–45)

Yet again Jesus insists to his reluctant disciples that his suffering and death is all one with the glory and majesty at which they marvel. The very moment when they are lost in admiration is the moment when they must be reminded of his passion to come, just as, earlier, the very moment of recognition was the moment of the first passion-prophecy, and the very moment of transfiguration was the moment of discussing his exodus. What for us seems a zig-zag pattern of joy and foreboding, is for Jesus a smooth and continual ascent towards the ecstasy of abandon into his Father's hands.

Abandon into his Father's hands was also abandon 'into the hands of men'. The word for 'delivered' here, also means 'betrayed', or, more literally, 'given over'. Judas, in 'betraying' Jesus, was 'giving over' something that did not belong to him, that he had no right to give — the life of the Son of man. But when Jesus 'gave *himself* over', 'delivered *himself* up', he was giving what was his to give. The death of Jesus was a gift of himself to the world. And, as we know, we give to those we love; we give most to those we love most; and we give our whole lives (as in marriage) to those we love beyond all measure.

So when Jesus warns that he will be given over into the hands of men, he is speaking of something both anguished and deeply joyful. The pain of the 'giving over' is real and terrible, for he will suffer both physical torture and the agony of moral betrayal by friends. But at the same time the 'giving over' is an act of self-gift, in which he has the joy of expressing his love for humanity, in a total, consummated way, and in a way that will bring us the fullness of salvation.

And in this giving, we have the joy of receiving. We receive salvation, but not just as an empty, abstract, meaningless concept. The salvation we receive is not a concept, but a person, a person we love, the person of Christ. When Jesus gives himself over into our hands, we cannot fail to feel deep thankfulness and union with him, even if that joy is all of a piece with the suffering.

This profound truth about the gift of Jesus' life was more than the disciples could understand at the time. They could not understand the joy of this promise, nor could they understand the misery of it. 'And they were afraid to ask him about this saying.' It is all very reminiscent of our feelings when we fear that we, or our loved ones, may be dying. This pain in the hip, this passing of blood, this growing weakness . . . Is it cancer? Is it death? We are afraid to ask.

And so, when Jesus spoke of being delivered into the hands of men, the disciples were afraid to ask. They tried not to hear when he told them he was going to die. They tried to think he was talking about something else. They tried to forget. They could not bear to lose him.

No more could we bear to lose him. We could not bear to live without Christ. But only now, in the post-resurrection era, can we, falteringly, understand that the crucified Christ is the Christ who is not taken from us, but given to us, to be ours, for ever.

Prayer As you gave yourself into the hands of men,
        help us to give ourselves into your hands.

. . . the Mount of Olives.

We have now finished the section of the gospel dealing with the transfiguration, and we move to the passion narrative itself, picking it up as Jesus leaves the Upper Room and goes to the Mount of Olives. Taking a few verses each day, the story of the passion will take us up to Easter.

And he came out, and went, as was his custom, to the Mount of Olives; and the disciples followed him.

(Luke 22:39)

' . . . and went, as was his custom'. We may only remember the name 'Mount of Olives' from this story of the agony in the garden, but it actually plays a more constant role in the narrative than that. When Jesus makes his triumphal entry into Jerusalem on the back of the donkey, he makes it from the Mount of Olives (Luke 19:28–40). That triumphal entry was of tremendous importance in the construction of the narrative, being prepared for by many earlier references to Jesus setting 'his face to go to Jerusalem' (Luke 9:51), 'journeying toward Jerusalem' (Luke 13:22), being 'on the way to Jerusalem' (Luke 17:11), saying 'Behold, we are going up to Jerusalem' (Luke 18:31), being 'near to Jerusalem' (Luke 19:11), and going 'on ahead, going up to Jerusalem' (Luke 19:28). Jesus' journey to Jerusalem is clearly the great journey of his life, preparing, as it did, for the consummation of his life on the cross.

The Mount of Olives, or Mount Olivet, is a sizeable place, with houses on it (where the colt was tied up), and a good stretch of road before the descent to Jerusalem begins (Luke 19:36–37). It was to the Mount of Olives that Jesus returned each night, after his daily ministry of teaching in the temple that marked his last, fateful visit to Jerusalem (Luke 21:37), but the place where he used to sleep was only one spot on the Mount — mentioned by name in Matthew and Mark as Gethsemane, referred to in John as 'a garden', and in Luke just 'the place' (in the coming verse 40). It was to Mount Olivet, again, that he would return for his ascension (Acts 1:12).

However, before arriving at the place of his agony we must follow Jesus — as 'the disciples followed him' — from Jerusalem to the Mount. It was a journey that Jesus had made so many times, and in the last days twice daily (once each way). Once he had made it in great triumph (his Palm Sunday entry), and once more to come he was to make it in ignominy and darkness, for the last time. Jesus goes out, on the road he knows so well, aware that his only purpose in going is to return again, after about three hours, and then under arrest.

It is not a long walk — only about a quarter of an hour. In Matthew and Mark there is a brief discourse on the road (again warning of his death but promising his resurrection) but in Luke's account there is no mention of teaching on the way.

What could his feelings have been? In a way it was a foreshadowing of the next journey out of Jerusalem, to the other mount — the mount of Calvary. This time the burden he had to bear was not on his back but in his heart.

So shortly before he had been sharing in a meal of love with his disciples. He had given his body and blood at that meal, anticipating the gift that was to be made on the cross. He was committed. It was only a matter of enduring another day, and it would be all over, finished, accomplished ('It is finished' — John 19:30). In some ways it must have been easier to endure those remaining hours with something simple to do, like walking, than alone on the Mount of Olives, with nothing to do but wait.

Prayer Let me walk with you, Jesus,
on the road to your passion.
Walk with me, Jesus,
along the roads of my life.

'. . . remove this cup.'

And when he came to the place he said to them, 'Pray that you may not enter into temptation.' And he withdrew from them about a stone's throw, and knelt down and prayed, 'Father, if thou art willing, remove this cup from me; nevertheless not my will, but thine, be done.' And there appeared to him an angel from heaven, strengthening him. And being in an agony he prayed more earnestly; and his sweat became like great drops of blood falling down upon the ground.

(Luke 22:40–44)

Jesus has longed to make a gift of his life for the world, but now he fears the dying. The pain that lies ahead is beyond imagination. Every time we think of the greatest pain conceivable, we have to answer 'no — it will be worse than that'. The agony is increased by the fact that his disciples will abandon him, Peter will deny him, the very crowd for whom he has spent himself in healing and teaching, will cry out for his blood. Hurt, rejection, failure, betrayal, misunderstanding, injustice, mockery and ingratitude will all be heaped onto a physical torture that is terrifying to contemplate.

And worst of all is that he has the choice. He could say 'no', even now, even though he has sacramentally committed himself in the institution of the eucharist. He could, even now, appeal to God to send 'more than twelve legions of angels' (Matthew 26:53).

When Sheila Cassidy was tortured in Chile, she asked her interrogators afterwards, 'Does everyone talk, or am I weak?' They answered, 'Everyone has their breaking point'. Here, on the Mount of Olives, Jesus seems at his breaking point. He can no longer say 'yes' to his passion. He can only say 'remove this cup from me'. But, mercifully, the sole thread by which he can hang on to his destiny is acceptance of the will of God. He can no longer say 'yes' to his passion, but he would never say 'no' to the will of God: 'Father, if thou art willing . . . nevertheless not my will, but thine, be done.'

The prayer he had taught his disciples long ago, on another mount — the Our Father — with its crucial phrase 'Thy will be done', has always been so deeply embedded in Jesus' heart and will that he can pray no other way. No matter how desperate his agony, so that his sweat falls like great drops of

blood, his cries for help always mingle with 'Thy will be done'. 'Remove this cup . . . nevertheless not my will, but thine, be done.'

The cup — the cup of his blood, pledged at the Last Supper — already begins to be filled, as his sweat falls readily, becoming 'like great drops of blood falling down'. For he does not just look ahead to his passion: his passion has begun.

Prayer Thy will be done.

. . . sleeping for sorrow.

And when he rose from prayer, he came to the disciples and found them sleeping for sorrow, and he said to them, 'Why do you sleep? Rise and pray that you may not enter into temptation.'

(Luke 22:45–46)

'Pray that you may not enter into temptation.' It is the second time Jesus makes this appeal to his disciples on this night (see verse 40), and it is a prayer that, like the 'Thy will be done', comes straight from the 'Our Father': 'Lead us not into temptation'.

The subsequent events explain what temptations Jesus had in mind. When the armed men arrive, the disciples start striking about with swords; when the servants ask Peter if he is a follower of Jesus, he denies it; Matthew and Mark speak of the cowardice of the disciples, who abandoned Jesus and fled as soon as he was arrested. It can all be summed up as a lack of faith — an inability to understand what kind of a Messiah Jesus was; a resistance to the will of God because it did not follow the lines that worldly reason dictated.

'Pray that you may not enter into temptation.' But they could not, over-whelmed as they were with heaviness of heart at Jesus' incomprehensible warnings about death and betrayal.

He 'found them sleeping for sorrow'. Our hearts go out to the disciples in their failure. Most of us know the experience of falling asleep at our prayers, failing even as we are doing our best to be present and alert in God's presence.

Most of us know the experience of being so tired that we cannot keep awake — of struggling to open and re-open the eyelids that slip down again and again, until, in a split-second of abandon, we let ourselves give up the battle, and fall straightaway into sleep.

And most of us know the experience of sorrow so great that sleep is a mercy, perhaps the only mercy. We know how often our sleep has been the only means of enduring a depression or finding relief from a tragedy; we know how each morning's waking has been a slip into a deeper pit than sleep, the pit of black memory. Shakespeare spoke of

> . . . the innocent sleep,
> Sleep that knits up the ravell'd sleave of care,
> The death of each day's life, sore labour's bath,
> Balm of hurt minds . . .
>
> (*Macbeth* 2:2:37–40)

When the disciples could not watch with Christ, but instead slept 'for sorrow', we feel very much with them. The best friend they had ever had, the saviour of all time, the most wonderful person the world had ever known, and, by the grace of God, their constant companion, the man whom they loved with a love they had never known before . . . was hourly drawing nearer his death. How could they not sleep 'for sorrow'?

And yet the message of Jesus was that, though this was cause for pain, it was not cause for depression. It was the greatest event of all time, and if the disciples could only have realized its importance, all desire for sleep would have been knocked out of their minds. If the disciples could only have realized what was going to happen, and how soon, and with what result, then sleep would have been as impossible as it is to the pregnant woman who, having gone to bed to sleep, finds suddenly her time of delivery is upon her, and she has many hours' labour to face before sleep will be possible again. And by the time she has been through her labour and delivered her baby, she will be unable to sleep for excitement.

Prayer Lead us not into temptation
but lead us into your prayer,
to say with you,
'Thy will be done'.

. . . he drew near to kiss him.

While he was still speaking, there came a crowd, and the man called Judas, one of the twelve, was leading them. He drew near to Jesus to kiss him; but Jesus said to him, 'Judas, would you betray the Son of man with a kiss?'

(Luke 22:47–48)

Luke makes us feel we are really there, especially if we translate the Greek more literally as 'while he was still speaking, look — a crowd'. We are maybe picking up the immediacy of an eye-witness account Luke has heard, rather than being treated to a bit of artificial, literary vividness.

We can share in that eye-witness immediacy if we let ourselves imagine the scene. We can put ourselves with Jesus on that Mount, and wait, and hear him say to us 'Why do you sleep? Rise and pray that you may not enter into temptation,' and, while he is still saying those words, we too can look and see a crowd.

We too can watch the crowd drawing close through the darkness of the night — the night that Jesus will shortly call 'your hour, and the power of darkness' (verse 53). We too can see them undeniably making for us and, by the light of their torches, we can see their swords and clubs. In the end we can see, by the eerie light of a burning lantern, the face of one of our closest friends — one of the twelve. Up till this moment not one of us had any idea that he was a traitor — the name of Judas had not yet become blackened. But now he comes with armed men, and we know why.

The 'kiss of Judas' has become famous as an image of painful betrayal. Luke draws particular attention to the kiss, for he is the only evangelist to record Jesus' reproach: 'Judas, would you betray the Son of man with a kiss?' And yet we are so used to thinking of Judas as the traitor that it is difficult to recapture the sense that this was betrayal not by an enemy, but by a friend.

There is no one who can hurt us as a friend can. If a jealous rival says nasty things about me, I am hardly surprised, and neither will be those who hear the stories. But if a close friend does the same, I am hurt and mystified, and do not know how to forget the incident, however hard I try. If I find that the man my wife is sleeping with is not someone unknown, but a friend to whom I have shown great kindness and trust, then my hurt is re-doubled. If I have

46

my purse stolen, and find that it was taken by the au pair whom I have trusted and liked, then I grieve inwardly for far more than the money.

And so with Judas, the friend of Jesus, who (in Matthew's gospel) Jesus even greets in Gethsemane as 'friend'. Undoubtedly Judas and Jesus loved each other. The kiss was a sign of the truth of that love, as well as a sign of the falsehood of betrayal. The tragedy was not just that someone had shown the chief priests where Jesus spent the night, but that one of the twelve, whom Jesus loved and trusted, had done so. The tragedy of betrayal by a friend, is that the past, which we thought was as solid as the ground we stand on, is dug up and shown to be full of holes.

Prayer   You know how I have been hurt by my friends.
Let me bury that hurt I feel
inside the hurt that you felt
when your friend betrayed you.

. . . cut off his right ear.

And when those who were about him saw what would follow, they said, 'Lord, shall we strike with the sword?' And one of them struck the slave of the high priest and cut off his right ear. But Jesus said, 'No more of this!' And he touched his ear and healed him.

(Luke 22:49–51)

There are times in our lives when we do something really stupid, so stupid that we can never afterwards remember it without profound embarrassment. This cutting off of the ear is one of those moments. Matthew, Mark and Luke all refrain from saying (or perhaps in the confusion their sources did not know) who did this stupid act. But John's gospel tell us it was Peter, and the name of the servant was Malchus.

At the time, however, it must have seemed a lot more reasonable than it did in retrospect. It is Luke who gives us Jesus' puzzling words about swords at the Last Supper — words that could easily have been taken to encourage armed resistance: 'let him who has no sword sell his mantle and buy one'. We might have expected Jesus to ban the carrying of swords, and we might have expected an answer to the question — 'Lord, shall we strike with the sword?' — before any damage was done.

The disciples were trying to preserve the Christ for his work of salvation, but they had not taken in what kind of a Christ Jesus was: one who would suffer and die and on the third day rise again. Only, it seems, when they saw the Judas-led crowd approaching with swords and clubs, did they realize that Jesus really would be arrested, and they feared what the outcome might be.

So they panicked and struck out. Often, when we do something really stupid, it passes almost unnoticed, and we can behave as though we had never done it. Unfortunately in this case an ear is chopped off. Considering the pain and disfigurement that involves, it is a great relief to be told that Jesus immediately healed it. (Luke alone tells us this.) The healing is not sufficient, however, for everyone to pretend the incident had never happened: it is recorded in scripture for ever after as one of the great mistakes that the faithful and well-intentioned can make.

Dear, great St Peter. All the more dear for being such a silly, impulsive ass

on occasions. There is hope for us all. But his biggest act of stupidity is still to come.

Prayer Christ, my Lord,
save me from my stupidity,
and heal the hurt caused by my mistakes.

. . . the power of darkness.

Then Jesus said to the chief priests and officers of the temple and elders, who had come out against him, 'Have you come out as against a robber, with swords and clubs? When I was with you day after day in the temple, you did not lay hands on me. But this is your hour, and the power of darkness.'

(Luke 22:52–53)

The arrest of Jesus may remind us of the swoop down on Solidarity, in Poland, one December night in 1981. In both cases the attack could not be in the open, in the light of day, for crowd pressure would have prevented it. In any case it was not a matter of arresting someone doing something illegal, but of removing people who were threatening because they spoke the truth fearlessly.

And so the chief priests choose a furtive time — the night; a furtive place — the secret garden where Jesus camped, outside Jerusalem; and furtive means — a gang of armed men. These are tactics that are sometimes required by the legal forces — when they have to arrest dangerous criminals. Jesus speaks in hurt, 'Have you come out against a robber, with swords and clubs?' From now on he will be treated as a common criminal.

'When I was with you day after day in the temple,' he continues, 'you did not lay hands on me.' The chief priests had not dared make their arrest when Jesus was in the midst of admiring crowds, although they had been wanting to for a long time (see Luke 19:47–48 and 20:19).

Often we take Jesus' side so automatically that we lose sight of the dilemma the chief priests found themselves in. Either they acted the way they did — trying to remove and destroy Jesus — or they had to put up with what he said, which meant accepting some very harsh criticisms indeed. Jesus used language against the scribes and Pharisees which constantly pushed them towards confrontation: 'Beware of the scribes, who like to go about in long robes, and love salutations in the market places and the best seats in the synagogues and the places of honour at feasts, who devour widows' houses and for a pretence make long prayers. They will receive the greater condemnation' (Luke 20:46–47).

The harshest words of all come in Matthew's gospel: 'Woe to you, scribes and Pharisees, hypocrites! for you are like whitewashed tombs, which outwardly appear beautiful, but within they are full of dead men's bones and all uncleanness . . . You serpents, you brood of vipers, how are you to escape being sentenced to hell?' (Matthew 23:27, 33).

It is not easy to accept you are as bad as that, especially if your entire self-identity relies on marks of respect and honour. Jesus gives them a radical challenge to repent, and to rethink their values. If they say yes, they will go through a deep and painful process of conversion; they will become very different people from what they were before.

But instead they choose to suppress Jesus — a decision that seemed the easier option at the time, but finally proved as impossible as turning the sun off its course. Their attempt to eliminate Jesus will only bring him back with greater power, authority and influence than ever before. The truth cannot be escaped indefinitely.

But for a little, they seem to have won. 'This is your hour, and the power of darkness.' Jesus draws attention to the fact that it is not good sense or prudent concern for the public good that is the victor. Falsehood or darkness is the victor — for the time being. And twelve hours or so later that point is made even more strongly by the eclipse of the sun during Jesus' last hours on the cross: 'there was darkness over the whole land until the ninth hour, while the sun's light failed' (Luke 23:44–45). A heavy shadow was cast over the chief priests' victory.

So a wrong decision, stubbornly taken, with eyes closed to the truth, and hearts closed to change, rebounds on us with its darkness, and brings us no relief.

Prayer When I have done wrong
give me courage to recognize the darkness of my choice
and to change my mind.

. . . Peter followed.

Then they seized him and led him away, bringing him into the high priest's house. Peter followed at a distance; and when they had kindled a fire in the middle of the courtyard and sat down together, Peter sat among them.

(Luke 22:54–55)

At each point in this narrative of the passion we are inclined to think 'So now it has really started'. And yet when the next stage begins it seems as though nothing so far has been anything more than preparatory. When Jesus was in agony in the garden we thought that the passion now was really beginning — and indeed it was. And yet when the crowd came, that seemed the real beginning. Now we read 'they seized him' — and that first act of violence on Jesus seems the marker of the passion proper. As each new step comes, no doubt we will go on feeling that up till now it has not been serious, compared with what is now starting, and we will probably go on thinking that until he is nailed on the cross: compared to that anything previous pales into insignificance.

But, for the time being, 'they seized him and led him away', and it is certainly the move to a new level, even if there are many more levels to climb before the summit of pain on the cross. Loss of freedom is one of the most dehumanizing experiences to live through, especially when accompanied by actual force: 'they seized him'. But Jesus was more than mere man: if it is dehumanizing for us what must it have been like for him? Of course the whole thing is crazy: a mad upside-down world, where for the time being evil triumphs. It is a nightmare, but it is not a dream: it is for real.

And he makes the journey again — the same journey, for the last time. In darkness he sees his beloved familiar world pass him for the last time — the world that he had so shortly before seen pass by the last light of evening, when he was still free. So many things now are for the last time. He has already eaten his last meal. He is living through his last night. His beloved friends are already scattering: which of them shall he see again, and in what circumstances?

The high priest's house should be — like the bishop's palace — a symbol of all that is good and true and holy. It should provide safe-keeping — as a criminal may find sanctuary by clinging to an altar. But tonight all our values will be overthrown.

And Peter followed — Peter who had said earlier that evening: 'Lord, I am ready to go with you to prison and to death.' So far he is trying to keep his word.

In the other gospels the assembly of chief priests meets by night; in Luke they wait till day comes (verse 66). It makes little odds — in either case the business is concluded by early morning, so that Jesus is led to Pilate at the beginning of the day. But in Luke's version the scene for Peter's denial is set far more poignantly: the crowd lead Jesus into the courtyard of the house, and keep him there under guard, taunting him. Peter enters into the same courtyard, sits by the same fire that warms the guard, and so (in verse 61) can be looked at directly by Jesus. We can imagine Jesus in one of the colder corners of the courtyard, surrounded by armed men — not of course Roman soldiers as yet; more likely tough guys that could be hired for rough work of this sort because it appealed to them. We can imagine a courtyard full of many people, with little light except from the fire. We can imagine Peter — frightened, trying to appear insignificant, trying to angle himself to get a look through the shadows at the far corner, trying to work out what to do, not knowing what to think, wondering what would happen, already aware that he had made a fool of himself on the Mount, deeply confused, and frightened, very frightened, knowing his attempt to stand up and fight heroically was a disaster, utterly baffled and desperately muddled. And now the waiting — and everything that happens now will be awful, everything spiralling in from disaster to disaster in an unstoppable vortex of tragedy.

Prayer This is the time when I begin to want to run away and give up.
Help me to stay with you through your passion, Jesus.
Help me to pray with you through this Lent.

'... Man, I am not.'

Then a maid, seeing him as he sat in the light and gazing at him, said, 'This man also was with him.' But he denied it, saying, 'Woman, I do not know him.' And a little later some one else saw him and said, 'You also are one of them.' But Peter said, 'Man, I am not.' And after an interval of about an hour still another insisted, saying, 'Certainly this man also was with him; for he is a Galilean.' But Peter said, 'Man, I do not know what you are saying.'

(Luke 22:56–60)

We have already set the scene, and imagined something of the inner turmoil Peter must have been in. Now we come to the greatest disaster of Peter's life — the time when he denied Christ, not once, but three times, and even then after being warned in advance.

Why should the man who would go 'to prison and to death' with Jesus, deny that he knew him? Once one has embarked on a mistaken course of action, it can be very difficult to extricate oneself, and instead one misjudgment leads to another. That is the awful tangle of human sin: it is self-perpetuating.

Peter's plan was probably to be something of a spy — to slip inside the enemy ranks so he could follow what happened to Jesus. In that way he would know what action, if any, was called for, or at least share in the sad knowledge of his fate by watching at a discreet distance, instead of having no idea what had happened to Jesus once he had been led off quietly into the night.

Up to a point it was an excellent plan. Perhaps we would not know even now of the blindfolding and mockery (verses 63–65) if someone (Peter, or another disciple — see John 18:15–16) had not slipped into the courtyard without revealing his identity as a disciple. (Only in Luke is this incident placed after Peter's exit from the courtyard.) But it is one thing to keep prudently silent, another to make a deliberate statement of dissociation from Jesus. Another possibility — and one that might well have appealed to Peter's temperament — would have been to hammer at the door crying, 'I am one of his disciples: take me as well'.

Peter's mistake began with his first denial — only then. It is impossible to know the balance of motivations that led Peter to this denial. Partly he would have justified it as a way of being able to stay to follow events — a way of being able to follow Jesus to nearer his death. But probably there was a large element of cowardice. Those who were mocking and beating up Jesus in the far corner would quite possibly have meted out similar treatment to a disciple who had been discovered infiltrating the ranks. It is easier to be heroic before you actually see what is happening to the person ahead of you.

John's gospel even adds the detail that the third accusation that Peter was a disciple came from a relative of the man whose ear Peter had cut off: that would give very good reason why Peter would have been frightened to reveal who he was.

Once the first denial had been made, the others followed — each more fearful, each more angry. According to Matthew and Mark, Peter ended up cursing and swearing that he knew nothing of Jesus. As we begin to realize we have made a mistake that is difficult to put right, we all tend to become more jumpy and angry with others. We are really angry with ourselves.

One of my favourite stories of St Peter comes not in the scriptures, but in handed-down tradition. Peter, it is said, was fleeing Rome during a persecution of Christians, and on the outskirts he met Jesus carrying his cross. 'Where are you going, Lord?' he asked. 'I am going to Rome to be crucified a second time,' came the answer. At once Peter realized that his imagined prudence was really cowardice. He turned and went straight back to Rome, and was crucified for his acknowledged faith in Christ — according to tradition, he asked to be crucified upside down because he was not worthy to die in exactly the same way as Jesus.

In that story Peter makes a similar, cowardly mistake, but he has the chance to put it right before it is too late. But in the courtyard of the high priest it is too late: not too late of course to be sorry, but too late to avoid making the denials that he has already spoken — denials that he once swore he would never make. 'Even if I must die with you, I will not deny you' (Matthew 26:35).

Prayer Help me to turn round and go back when I have made a mistake.
Help me to say sorry.

. . . the Lord turned and looked at Peter.

And immediately, while he was still speaking, the cock crowed. And the Lord turned and looked at Peter. And Peter remembered the word of the Lord, how he had said to him, 'Before the cock crows today, you will deny me three times.' And he went out and wept bitterly.

(Luke 22:60–62)

The crowing of the cock, that should be the joyful herald of the new dawn, is here the ominous confirmation of the blackness of the night and of the darkness of sin.

'And the Lord turned and looked at Peter.' Only Luke's account tells us of this painful exchange of glances — the last time Peter saw Jesus before his death. Of course Jesus must have understood what led Peter to deny him so disastrously. In a way that must have made it worse. This was not a look that sprang from misunderstanding and misinformation. It was the look of the man he loved in the moment when he had denied loving him. It was the look of the man he had wounded, in the moment of his pain.

After all, Jesus had not urged Peter to promise fidelity. It was Peter who insisted on it. His denial shows himself so lacking in self-knowledge that he will not know what trust he can ever place in himself again. From now on he must learn to place his trust not in *his* love, *his* fidelity, *his* strength, but only in the Lord. Jesus will not disown Peter, nor punish him — except by letting Peter see himself as he is. After his resurrection he will not even rub in the infidelity by saying 'I forgive you': better than that, he gives Peter a new chance to speak his love. 'Simon, son of John, do you love me?' (John 21:16). And even in advance, he has assured him that he can get over this sin — he need not be crushed by it. 'I have prayed for you that your faith may not fail; and when you have turned again, strengthen your brethren' (Luke 22:32).

What Peter has done for us, in this denial, is enabled us to see what a serious sin denial of Christ is. In the early Church apostasy — or denial of Christ — was one of the three classic mortal sins, along with murder and adultery. The Church has never held that if threatened with torture and death it was all right to tell lies about our Christian allegiance. Readiness to face death for the sake of faith in Christ is what being a Christian means. Christian faith is on a totally different level from any other sort of conviction or belief. There are few things, in the end, worth dying for, but commitment to Christ is one of them.

And so Peter was the first apostate. 'And he went out and wept bitterly.' It was not a mistake he would make again. For Peter showed us not only what a serious sin it is to deny Christ, but also how painful it is to realize how we have sinned. He wept bitterly because he had stupidly and needlessly been unfaithful to the man he loved, and hurt him; but his love for Jesus enabled him to feel Jesus' pain and weep because he had caused it.

Peter's grief was pure repentance. He did not weep because he had been punished, or because he was afraid what would happen to him, or because someone had told him he ought to repent. He wept simply because he saw what he had done. If we suffer for our sins after death it must be for the same reason — not that God heaps fires and punishments on us, but simply that we see what we have done.

What a gentle grace is this gift of knowing our sins! It would have been easy for Jesus to leave Peter in his illusions, thinking he was the brave, faithful follower. Instead he lets him see straightaway — with the crowing of the cock — the way he had behaved: you said this, and now you have done that. The knowledge is a painful gift, but a gift all the same. Without it there can be no progress.

Prayer Give me the gift, Jesus,
of seeing what I have done.

'... Prophesy!'

Now the men who were holding Jesus mocked him and beat him; they also blindfolded him and asked him, 'Prophesy! Who is it that struck you?' And they spoke many other words against him, reviling him.

(Luke 22:63–65)

It seems from the gospel accounts that Jesus was mocked and beaten both by the high priest's men, and by Pilate's soldiers (although Luke does not mention the latter). It was Pilate's soldiers who put on him the crown of thorns and the purple robe (Matthew 27:27–30; Mark 15:16–19; John 19:2–3), but the mockery in the high priest's house seems similar in style, if less sophisticated. Matthew, Mark and John suggest that Jesus was struck during or after the trial before the Sanhedrin, but Luke (who postpones that trial until early morning) sees the mockery going on through the night.

Throughout his ministry Jesus showed commanding authority. He won arguments, he saw traps laid for him, he escaped from the thick of crowds, he attracted adulation.

Now, in his passion, he acts differently. He lets himself be hit repeatedly, when in his typical style he could have shamed his attackers with a few words that spoke to their hearts. He lets himself be blindfolded, although he was the only one with any true vision in the blind darkness of that night. We cannot imagine him answering their challenge to prophesy who struck him, although such a game would have been child's play to him. If he did not answer they would have hit him more and more to try and force an answer out of him. But for Jesus, power is a force to be used for healing, where there is faith; it is not a trump card for scoring points off unbelievers.

And so Jesus enters more deeply into the pain of humanity — not just the ordinary human pains of hunger and tiredness, of being misunderstood and rejected. He now enters into the unsightedness and inarticulacy and ineffectiveness of the least gifted among us. He simply suffers, without any kind of response, and because he makes no response he is hit and hit again.

Prayer Forgive me, Jesus, for the times when
I have attacked people because they were stupid,
or hurt people because they could not hurt me back.

'. . . If you are the Christ, tell us.'

When day came, the assembly of the elders of the people gathered together, both chief priests and scribes; and they led him away to their council, and they said, 'If you are the Christ, tell us.' But he said to them, 'If I tell you, you will not believe; and if I ask you, you will not answer. But from now on the Son of man shall be seated at the right hand of the power of God.' And they all said, 'Are you the Son of God, then?' And he said to them, 'You say that I am.' And they said, 'What further testimony do we need? We have heard it ourselves from his own lips.'

(Luke 22:66–71)

The long series of trials begins. After this council, there will be Pilate, Herod, and a long, long session with Pilate again.

In some ways this meeting of the priests and elders must have been the most painful of all. To be misunderstood and misjudged by bad men, or men of worldly interests, is hardly surprising. But this assembly of elders of the people was the highest possible religious authority by which Jesus could be judged — short of God himself. To be condemned by those who have been chosen as men of high learning and personal sanctity, by those who are respected and revered by the people of God, by those who hold in trust the preservation of the true faith . . . that is a hurt that cannot be described. It makes one feel one is going mad, and there is enormous pressure to say, 'Well, perhaps I was wrong . . . perhaps at least I handled it badly . . .'

That is why we sometimes hear it said today, in pain: 'To suffer for the Church is one thing, but to suffer at the hands of the Church is quite another.'

The discussion in council echoes, sinisterly, the beautiful days of freedom around the time of the transfiguration. 'If you are the Christ, tell us,' they demand, and Jesus cannot say yes, not because he is not the Christ, but because it has to be a recognition that people make for themselves. If he told them he was the Christ, they would not believe it, and why, in a sense, should they, on the basis of his own testimony? If someone told us 'I am the greatest composer of the century', or 'I am the best man to be your member of Parliament', we would be suspicious: they have to wait for us to find out for ourselves. And so we remember the blessed moment near the mount of the

60

transfiguration when Jesus did not tell who he was, but rather asked: 'Who do you say that I am?' And Peter answered, 'The Christ of God' (Luke 9:20).

And there is an echo, also, when Jesus says, 'From now on the Son of man shall be seated at the right hand of the power of God.' It is the last part — the last glorious part — of the prophecy of the passion, now taken alone as a final note of hope. Could it be as much a way of keeping hold of his own hope and purpose, as a message for the elders? It is the truth, but the last bit of the truth he needs to hold onto, while he is plunged through the earlier parts of suffering he has foretold. We remember how he immediately answered Peter's act of faith in Jesus as 'the Christ of God', with the foreboding words, 'The Son of man must suffer many things, and be rejected by the elders and chief priests and scribes, and be killed, and on the third day be raised'.

'And they all said, "Are you the Son of God, then?" ' We can cast our minds back to the transfiguration, and the word of God on the mountain: 'This is my Son, my Chosen.' We know so clearly the answer to these questions. Yes, Jesus is the Christ. Yes, he is the Son of God. They are truths screaming for recognition, sacredly confirmed in the intimate group of disciples in the earlier days of ministry, implicitly accepted by the crowds that flocked round Jesus in the temple, and now held up in challenge by the chief priests for Jesus to affirm or deny. What should be a holy moment of faith is dragged through the dirt of a court, and submitted to the analyses of lawyers.

The elders do not get the clear answer they are looking for, but they seize on Jesus' evasive words, 'You say that I am', as though he had said, 'I am what you say', and announce the charge is proved. It grates to hear Jesus condemned on the charge of claiming to be who he really is. If there is blasphemy, it is not Jesus who is the blasphemer.

Prayer You are the Christ.
Help me to say it in the way Peter did,
lovingly and trustingly.
You are the Son of God.
Help me to hear it said in the way the disciples heard it,
with awe and reverence.

'. . . Are you the King of the Jews?'

Then the whole company of them arose, and brought him before Pilate. And they began to accuse him, saying, 'We found this man perverting our nation, and forbidding us to give tribute to Caesar, and saying that he himself is Christ a king.' And Pilate asked him, 'Are you the King of the Jews?' And he answered him, 'You have said so.' And Pilate said to the chief priests and the multitudes, 'I find no crime in this man.' But they were urgent, saying, 'He stirs up the people, teaching throughout all Judea, from Galilee even to this place.'

(Luke 23:1–5)

In this picture one of the chief priests seems to be counting off on his fingers the charges against Jesus. How could we answer them?

'We found this man perverting our nation . . . He stirs up the people, teaching throughout all Judea, from Galilee even to this place.' Yes, Jesus did stir up the people, in a sense. They flocked to him, because he healed the sick and taught them the truth about the love of God. In the course of doing that he had to make some very unpleasant and strongly worded criticisms. Is that what is called 'perverting the nation'?

'. . . forbidding us to give tribute to Caesar . . . ' Jesus had not said that, but rather 'Render to Caesar the things that are Caesar's, and to God the things that are God's' (Luke 20:25). It may well be that many people who made too strong a link between Jesus and the sort of nationalistic, freedom-fighting Messiah they were looking for, might have thought Jesus would be opposed to paying the tribute. It might even be that, inspired by the hope of a free nation under Jesus, they would have begun to withhold it. But it certainly was not what Jesus meant, or what he said.

'. . . and saying that he himself is Christ a king.' But Jesus had spent his entire ministry trying to shut up people who recognized who he was. So much did he do this that the biblical scholars are perplexed at all this emphasis on the 'messianic secret'. Yes, he was Christ. Yes, in a sense he was a king. But he never went around saying so. If he stirred up the people it was not because he told them he was Christ a king, but because they could not fail to recognize it.

Prayer You are the Christ.
        You are my king.
        I recognize you.

... he made no answer.

When Pilate heard this, he asked whether the man was a Galilean. And when he learned that he belonged to Herod's jurisdiction, he sent him over to Herod, who was himself in Jerusalem at that time. When Herod saw Jesus, he was very glad, for he had long desired to see him, because he had heard about him, and he was hoping to see some sign done by him. So he questioned him at some length; but he made no answer. The chief priests and the scribes stood by, vehemently accusing him.

(Luke 23:6–10)

Only Luke recounts this dramatic meeting between Jesus and Herod. Herod, we learn from earlier in Luke's gospel, had done many evil things, including marrying his brother's wife, Herodias, and imprisoning John the Baptist because he had reproached him for it (Luke 3:19–20). Later he beheaded John the Baptist (Luke 9:9), and was said to be planning to kill Jesus as well (Luke 13:31). Jesus called him 'that fox' (Luke 13:32).

Now Jesus walks straight into the jaws of 'that fox', under arrest, plus a battery of chief priests and scribes to help Herod find every excuse to execute him. And yet Herod does not kill Jesus, despite their determination. Perhaps Herod does not like being told what to do.

What sort of signs might Herod have asked for? 'Turn this into gold', or 'Make this stick flower', or 'Come now, I do not believe you have any powers at all.' Perhaps 'I will have you beheaded unless you . . . ' Every attempt to elicit a sign fails, whether by flattery or threats. Jesus remains silent. As the poignant prophecy from Isaiah says:

He was oppressed, and he was afflicted,
yet he opened not his mouth;
like a lamb that is led to the slaughter,
and like a sheep that before its shearers is dumb,
so he opened not his mouth.

(Isaiah 53:7)

Silence can sometimes speak louder than words. It was said of Thomas More, when he refused to take the oath of supremacy that recognized Henry VIII as head of the Church in England — refused to say what he thought one way or the other — 'This silence of his is bellowing up and down Europe'.

Silence is so close to prayer that we can almost say silence *is* prayer. It can be the silence of mutual enjoyment, when we enjoy the presence of God without needing to say a word. Or it can be the silence of accepted suffering, when we do not tense up against the pain, but open ourselves in an act of self-giving. It is that silence that is Jesus' silence now — a silence in which he gathers all his faculties into an act of tranquil self-giving to God.

The silence of Jesus in his passion is captured in many works of art, including the engravings in this book. There is his sad face as Judas comes up to kiss him (see p. 49), or his silence before the taunts to 'prophesy!' (see p. 59), or his heavy sorrow before the cackle of accusers (here), or his stretched-out agony on the cross (see p. 95), or his dead limbs falling in total self-giving as he was carried to the tomb (see p. 99).

Prayer Let me share in your silence, Lord.

. . . and mocked him.

And Herod with his soldiers treated him with contempt and mocked him; then, arraying him in gorgeous apparel, he sent him back to Pilate. And Herod and Pilate became friends with each other that very day, for before this they had been at enmity with each other.

(Luke 23:11–12)

In Luke's version it is Herod's soldiers, not Pilate's, who taunt Jesus, dressing him up like a mock king. Little is said of the details here, but Matthew, Mark and John give fuller accounts, though the order of events seems to be different. If we put the accounts together, the mockery might have gone like this.

Jesus was led inside the palace. Then the soldiers called together their whole cohort to take part in the mockery — that is, between two hundred and six hundred infantrymen. It seems unlikely, but that is what the texts say. At least it must have been more than the four or five we customarily think of.

Next they strip Jesus. Then they dress him in a scarlet (or purple) robe: this might have been one of the red cloaks that formed part of the soldiers' uniform, or it might (as Luke perhaps suggests) have been something more lavish. They make a crown by plaiting together thorn branches, and put it on his head. (The Roman emperor is shown on coins of the period wearing a crown with radiant spikes, and if evidence from the Turin Shroud is accepted, it was a cap covering the head and causing a dozen or more wounds that bled freely; one of the trickles of blood wavered in its course down Jesus' forehead as it met the furrows of his brow in a reflex contraction of pain.)

As well as the 'royal' robe and the crown of thorns, they gave Jesus a stick for a sceptre in his right hand. They came up and knelt before Jesus (perhaps a long line of mock subjects), saying 'Hail, King of the Jews', imitating the reverence shown to the Roman emperor, who was not only a king but also treated as god. Then they spat at Jesus, and hit him about the head with the stick he was holding.

According to Matthew and Mark, all this happened after the sentence of death and scourging. According to John, the mockery is still after the scourging, but before the death sentence. But Luke, who alone records the meeting with Herod, places the mockery and the clothing in kingly robes at this earlier point. In any case this mockery of Jesus as a king, by soldiers, can be distinguished from the earlier mockery of him as a prophet, in the high priest's house.

We can suppose that the soldiers found this mockery enjoyable. Most of us take certain relish in doing down other people, particularly the successful and powerful about whom we feel a certain jealousy. Usually we do people down by talking about them behind their backs rather than by hitting them in the face.

The game may have provided a certain release for feelings of resentment they had against their own bosses — whether Herod, or Pilate, or the emperor. Most of us feel resentment against those in charge of us, and enjoy the chance to complain about them. It may be the boss at work, or the management of a company. It may be the prime minister and the government. It may be the authorities of the Church. All of these need to be criticized fearlessly and honestly. But when we can feel ourselves laying it on with relish, joining a sea of angry voices, without the willingness to see merits and good intentions if they are there, then we share in the action of the soldiers towards Jesus. We set someone up as a king in order to attack him for it.

Jesus is sent back to Pilate. He has now been through three trials, but more battling about his fate is still to come.

Prayer I want to think I am not like the soldiers.
Help me to see the ways in which I share their sin.

'... I will therefore chastise him.'

Pilate then called together the chief priests and the rulers and the people, and said to them, 'You brought me this man as one who was perverting the people; and after examining him before you, behold, I did not find this man guilty of any of your charges against him; neither did Herod, for he sent him back to us. Behold, nothing deserving death has been done by him; I will therefore chastise him and release him.' Now he was obliged to release one man to them at the festival.

(Luke 23:13–17)

It is easier to visualize this scene if we take note of information given in John's gospel: the Jews did not enter Pilate's palace, 'so that they might not be defiled, but might eat the passover' (John 18:28). So Pilate comes in and out, perhaps speaking to the chief priests and surrounding crowd from a balcony. Sometimes he goes out alone (John 18:29, 38), and sometimes he brings Jesus with him (John 19:5; 19:13). This succession of disputes between Pilate and the crowd is recorded in Luke as a threefold struggle, of which today's reading represents the first round. Three times Pilate says he will release Jesus. Three times the crowd cry out demanding his death. For Jesus the whole incident must have been extremely draining, with increasing mental strain as he awaited the inevitable sentence.

Pilate finds Jesus innocent of the charge of perverting the nation — connected, as it had been, with the charges of encouraging tax-evasion and setting himself up as a king in opposition to the Roman emperor (Luke 23:2). But as a concession to the Jewish feelings of outrage he proposes to 'chastise' Jesus. What 'chastising' meant was scourging, and a Roman scourging was a terrible prospect. We know from the other gospels (it is not explicit in Luke) this scourging was eventually carried out — in Matthew and Mark after the death sentence had been given, but in John at this point, as an attempt to satisfy the crowd's bloodthirsty demands. From the first mention of 'chastising' we may imagine that Jesus felt sick from physical fear.

A combination of archaeological evidence, and Christian tradition, with illustration from the Shroud markings, enables us to reconstruct the scourging as follows. Perhaps not every detail is accurate, but at least the savagery of the instrument is confirmed by our knowledge of Roman weapons.

Jesus was chained to a pillar, probably with both hands up above his head. The impact and pain of the blows would surely have caused him to collapse if he had not been tied up in some way. Two soldiers took up position on either side, with Jesus' back towards them. They were armed with the *flagrum*, a stick with three thongs coming from the top, at the end of each of which were two small, lead balls. In other words, with each blow Jesus was struck by six metal pellets. Jesus received something like forty such blows. They landed all the way down his back and legs, and sometimes the thongs whipped round onto his chest and the front of his thighs. Every blow by the lead balls left a discernible weal.

And so, even as Pilate is landed with the surprising task of fighting for Jesus' life, his words are frightening. Jesus is led to and fro, from one palace to another, inside and outside the building, and the air is full of the threat of violence. So far we have heard of 'death' and of 'chastising' — both of them mild words for the tortures to come.

Prayer When I feel tension and fear
 I ask to be with you, Jesus,
 in your courage and peace.

'. . . crucify him!'

But they all cried out together, 'Away with this man, and release to us Barabbas' — a man who had been thrown into prison for an insurrection started in the city, and for murder. Pilate addressed them once more, desiring to release Jesus; but they shouted out, 'Crucify, crucify him!' A third time he said to them, 'Why, what evil has he done? I have found in him no crime deserving death; I will therefore chastise him and release him.' But they were urgent, demanding with loud cries that he should be crucified. And their voices prevailed.

(Luke 23:18–23)

Discussion and argument have broken down. Pilate tries to continue on a rational basis, but the crowd, incited by the high priests, resorts to mass demonstration, bordering on riot. It is Matthew who makes this most plain: 'a riot was beginning' (Matthew 27:24).

Pilate clearly did not like having his authority disregarded in the acquittal he had given to Jesus, but he disliked even more the threat to his authority if the riot went ahead. He decides the issue is not worth fighting over any more. 'And their voices prevailed.'

Jesus is terrifyingly alone. It is easy to forget this, looking back through the perspective of the Christian Church. It is easy to forget that he did not have us all standing by his side in that moment. He did not even have his own apostles supporting him, who, according to Matthew and Mark, had all abandoned him and fled. And according to all sources, one of his closest followers had betrayed him, and another had denied him.

As Jesus stood on that balcony with Pilate, hearing the mass of voices, seeing the swell of hatred rise against him, who was there to say a word in his defence? Could all these people shouting for his death be dismissed as evildoers? How was it possible for Jesus to hold together the undeniable inner knowledge that he was right, with the overwhelming external evidence that he was wrong — the unanimous, bellowed evidence of the crowd that he was not the Son of man, given for them, saving them, loved by them . . . but a dangerous, hated, rejected enemy?

He must have remembered how he had wept over Jerusalem earlier in his ministry: 'O Jerusalem, Jerusalem, killing the prophets and stoning those who are sent to you! How often would I have gathered your children together as a hen gathers her brood under her wings, and you would not!' (Luke 13:34). And again, as he made his Palm Sunday entry: 'And when he drew near and saw the city he wept over it, saying, "Would that even today you knew the things that make for peace!"' (Luke 19:41–42).

Here were the people he loved, the people he had wept over, the people he would die for, and they are crying out that he is more dangerous to them than a murderer. They choose Barabbas in preference to him.

We have often seen — in demonstrations or at football matches — the way that crowds shout their demands. A leader cries out a word or short phrase, and it is picked up with pounding rhythm by the crowd. Sometimes the people sway in unison, as a further sign of their unity. Sometimes they beat out their demands in the air with their clenched fists. It is difficult to resist being drawn into the strength of mass feeling like that. All four gospels tell us what that crowd cry was, that we can imagine beaten out with pounding rhythm: 'Crucify him. Crucify him. Crucify him.' They knew, and Jesus knew, what disgrace and torture lay in crucifixion. They could not have cried out any words that would have been more loaded with hatred and evil. And it all fell on Jesus, alone.

Prayer   I want to reach out to you,
         in your loneliness,
         and in your pain,
         as the fingers point at you.

. . . Jesus he delivered up.

So Pilate gave sentence that their demand should be granted. He released the man who had been thrown into prison for insurrection and murder, whom they asked for; but Jesus he delivered up to their will.

(Luke 23:24–25)

There is an awful finality about these two brief verses. The gospel simply states what happens, without judgment or emotion. And the simple truth cuts like a knife. ' . . . but Jesus he delivered up to their will.'

This is the point where Matthew and Mark place the scourging and the mockery. For John, it has already happened. And for Luke, as we have already noted, the mockery is in the hands of Herod's soldiers, and the scourging possibly in the intervals of Pilate's debate with the crowd.

There is a symbolic point made in the crowd's choice of Barabbas as the prisoner to be freed. As they choose a murderer (instead of Jesus) they become themselves murderers (of Jesus). They make unrighteous killing their free choice, in two senses.

And there is an irony in the fact that Barabbas actually was guilty of just the crimes Jesus is accused of — stirring up the people, perverting the nation, threatening the rule of Caesar. For Barabbas, we are told, was a man of revolutionary violence, guilty of sedition (or riot) and murder. Nothing could make it clearer that Jesus was not condemned for offences he had committed, but rather for the sort of person he was, and the strong reactions he provoked.

' . . . but Jesus he delivered up to their will.' There is a wealth of meaning in that single word 'delivered'. The Greek word to 'deliver', or 'give up', is used especially frequently in connection with the passion. Judas delivered Jesus to the chief priests (as in Matthew 26:15); the chief priests delivered Jesus to Pilate (as in Matthew 27:2); and now Pilate delivers Jesus up to their will (Luke 23:25). It is the same verb used every time.

And the same Greek verb is also used, positively, of God's giving up of his Son: 'He who did not spare his own Son but gave him up for us all, will he not also give us all things with him?' (Romans 8:32); and of Jesus' giving up of his own life: 'the Son of God, who loved me and gave himself for me' (Galatians 2:20).

72

The death of Jesus was not a meaningless accident, but a great act of giving. Some participated in the act wrongfully — giving away Jesus, giving him over into the hands of sinful men. But there was a great, saving meaning behind his death nonetheless, because it was also an act of self-giving, of rightful surrender and of loving generosity.

We have to participate in this process of giving in a just and loving way — not delivering up in a treacherous sense what is not ours to give — but giving ourselves freely and totally into God's hands, as he gave his Son freely and totally into our hands. As Paul writes (again using the same verb): 'While we live we are always being given up to death for Jesus' sake, so that the life of Jesus may be manifested in our mortal flesh' (2 Corinthians 4:11).

Today Pilate delivers up Jesus to death, and to the will of the chief priests. But today, too, God delivers up his Son, who freely gives himself, as a gift to us. We may not understand such love, we may be baffled, and wish it did not have to be this way. We may feel uncomfortable at the idea of a God who wants to make such excessive acts of self-sacrifice. But we cannot help being moved by the generosity of God, and challenged by it.

We may want to cry out with pain at the act of wrongful giving up by Pilate; or to cry out with joy at the act of loving giving by God; or to cry out for help in our weakness and unresponsiveness, now we have such an example of what generosity really means.

Prayer Help me to give myself to you
as you gave yourself to me.

... to carry it behind Jesus.

And as they led him away, they seized one Simon of Cyrene, who was coming in from the country, and laid on him the cross, to carry it behind Jesus.

(Luke 23:26)

The Way of the Cross has a firm and ancient place in Christian devotion. And yet the gospels say practically nothing about that journey. Luke has more than the others, because he has the meeting with the daughters of Jerusalem that we shall look at tomorrow. But apart from that, we are just told that Jesus was led out, and that Simon of Cyrene carried his cross. John's gospel contradicts this, and says that Jesus was led out, carrying his own cross.

The traditional explanation, which sounds perfectly plausible, is that Jesus began carrying his own cross but after a while the soldiers realized that, being weak from the scourging, he would not make it to Calvary without help. The fact that Jesus needed help does seem to confirm the severity of the scourging. We remember that Luke does not explicitly mention that the scourging was carried out, but everything seems to indicate that it was.

Traditional art shows Jesus carrying the whole cross, but modern scholarship tells us it was only the cross-bar. The upright post remained fixed securely in the ground, while the cross-bar was renewed for each victim: the prisoners carried their own cross-bars, lay on the ground to be nailed to them, and were then hoisted up to be suspended to the cross upright.

Christian tradition has tended to see Simon of Cyrene's carrying of the cross as an act of devoted service, as he relieves a little of Jesus' suffering. There is even, today, a group called the Cyrenians, who run hostels for down-and-outs; these are called Simon Houses, in memory of Simon's act of service. But how might the real Simon of Cyrene have felt about it?

Cyrene is in Northern Africa, some five hundred miles away from Jerusalem. We need not imagine that when Luke says Simon of Cyrene 'was coming in from the country' he meant that he had just arrived at Jerusalem on foot from Cyrene — which would have taken him the best part of a month — though I suppose it is not out of the question. Simon could have been a Jewish convert, resident in Judea, who had come, say, a day or two's journey for the Passover. At last he is on the road into Jerusalem, with the gates of the city open just before his eyes. In five minutes, he thinks, he will be inside the city. In half an hour, perhaps less, he will have found a lodging and can lie down and rest.

At this moment some Roman soldiers seize him, tie a heavy beam on his shoulders, and tell him to turn round and walk back in the other direction. The walk is uphill, up to the top of Mount Calvary. He is performing the same work as the most dangerous of condemned criminals. And when he gets to Calvary he may find the distasteful work of nailing human beings to wooden posts already under way. It must have been just about the most unwelcome end to his journey that he could have imagined.

And yet, and yet . . . He had come for the celebration of the old covenant, but now will be present at the consummation of the New Covenant. He had come to worship God in the temple, but now can worship God at the foot of the cross. He had come to make an act of religious service in attending the temple liturgy, but now can make a deeply privileged and unrepeatable act of service for Jesus, the Christ. Simon must be the patron saint of plans going wrong, and turning out differently and better. In the moment when our plans are completely overthrown, we can find the real religious moment we were deeply searching for — if we can let ourselves learn.

Just very gently, Luke hints at this new meaning found by Simon, for he carries the cross 'behind Jesus'. He follows Jesus. He becomes a follower of Jesus.

And Mark gives us another, equally gentle clue. Simon of Cyrene, 'the father of Alexander and Rufus' (Mark 15:21), he says. How on earth should Mark know the names of his children, or think that anyone else would have the slightest interest in knowing the names of his children, had not Simon, and Alexander and Rufus, become members of the believing community? It is as though Mark is saying 'Do you know Alexander and Rufus? Well it was their father who carried the cross.' This is mere hypothesis, but it is an intriguing thought, and supports the traditional interpretation that Simon knew himself privileged to carry the cross.

Prayer When my plans go wrong
       help me see
       that your plan for me is a better one.

'... Daughters of Jerusalem.'

And there followed him a great multitude of the people, and of women who bewailed and lamented him. But Jesus turning to them said, 'Daughters of Jerusalem, do not weep for me, but weep for yourselves and for your children. For behold, the days are coming when they will say, "Blessed are the barren, and the wombs that never bore, and the breasts that never gave suck!" Then they will begin to say to the mountains, "Fall on us"; and to the hills, "Cover us." For if they do this when the wood is green, what will happen when it is dry?'

(Luke 23:27–31)

According to at least three of the gospels, the group that followed Jesus to Calvary was predominantly made up of women. Matthew and Mark have already told us that 'all the disciples forsook him and fled' (Matthew 26:56), but they presumably meant the male disciples, especially the apostles, for the same gospels tell us that at the death there were 'many women there, looking on from afar, who had followed Jesus from Galilee' (Matthew 27:55).

The fidelity and courage of these women (it takes a strong stomach to witness a crucifixion) is a moving example to us. And then we can remember that in all four gospels the first Easter witnesses were women.

There is a slight puzzle in that the women addressed here are not, as later appear, 'women who had followed him from Galilee' (Luke 23:49) but rather 'daughters of Jerusalem'. Could Galilean women be described, by virtue of their Judaism that was centred in the temple, as 'daughters of Jerusalem'? Or perhaps we are dealing with two groups — the female Galileans, and the Jerusalem women.

Jesus' attention to the grief of these women bears a message about the unity of Christ and the world in one single cosmic tragedy. It is not as though everything, bar the condemnation of Jesus, was fine; it is not as though the world apart from him was at rights with itself. It might have seemed so, superficially, but Jesus denies that impression, and warns that the fate that now strikes him will soon strike others. 'Do not weep for me, but weep for yourselves and for your children.' (The sack of Jerusalem came about in A.D.70.)

The women have shown themselves at one with Jesus in choosing to share his grief. He shows himself at one with them, in revealing that his suffering is an anticipation of a tragedy that holds everyone in its grip.

What this means for us today, is that the awful sufferings of this world are united with Christ, and are all part of his passion in some mystical sense. The famines, the genocides, the war-shattered territories, the natural disasters ... over all these Jesus weeps. In the pain of all these, Jesus takes his share.

In this terrible and united grief, in which not a word of comfort can be spoken, Jesus shows the compassion, in the midst of his own passion, to see the impending pain of others, and to grieve for it. In grieving for the daughters of Jerusalem he shows compassion for all those who have died in war, those who are refugees, those who suffer and die from hunger, those in prison, including prisoners of conscience, and all those who suffer innocently.

Prayer In my mind I follow you, Jesus, on the Way of the Cross.
        You are condemned to death.
        You are given the cross.
        You fall for the first time.
        You meet your mother.
        Simon of Cyrene carries your cross.
        Veronica wipes your face.
        You fall for the second time.
        You meet the daughters of Jerusalem.
        You fall for the third time.
        You are stripped of your garments.
        You are nailed to the cross.
        You die on the cross.
        You are taken down from the cross.
        You are laid in the tomb.

. . . who were criminals.

Two others also, who were criminals, were led away to be put to death with him.

(Luke 23:32)

Jesus is led out with criminals, and shares the same fate as those who are so dangerous, so hated and despised by everyone, that it is felt necessary to inflict on them public torture and humiliation. Matthew and Mark tell us that the criminals were robbers — not great revolutionaries or anything noble like that, but probably really brutal, violent men who would be a threat to any society.

It is hard for us to remember this, because for us the crucifixion has become a noble image. We have to make a conscious effort to recall that at the time all the associations of being led away for crucifixion were of shame and disgrace. The appalling tortures that were to come are matched by the revulsion that people feel for the appalling deeds of the criminals. Public execution is partly a way of threatening others who might be tempted to the same crimes, and partly a way of expressing society's desire to spew this poisonous person out in total rejection.

Jesus is to be spewed out like that. He was made 'to be sin who knew no sin' (2 Corinthians 5:21). The final word on his life was to be 'criminal'.

How must Jesus have felt, knowing that he had called us to follow him, and finding that following him meant the way of the cross? Would not any leader, if his cause led him to crucifixion, turn round and tell his followers to go back, to escape this fate? Would not any reasonable man say 'no matter how just our cause, it is not worth it'? Crucifixion was designed to be so horrific as to leave no one in any doubt about that. Spartacus, the leader of the slave revolt, was crucified. Who would dare revolt after that?

As Jesus was led away for crucifixion, could he still have turned back to us followers and said again: 'Sell all that you have . . . and come, follow me' (Luke 18:22)? He could, but it is a terrifying thought. If we really love someone, it can be as bad to see them suffer, as to suffer ourselves. It hurts Jesus as much to see us in pain after him, as it does for him to suffer pain himself. And so the Christ who was led away, suffering, carried our sufferings with him; he suffered for us; our sufferings became united with his, and we weep for each other.

Jesus is given the same fate as criminals, and yet Luke phrases it in such a way that a new perspective is given. He does not write 'Jesus was led away with two others, who were criminals', as though Jesus becomes like the criminals. He writes instead, 'Two others also, who were criminals, were led away to be put to death with him,' as though the criminals become like Jesus. Through the death of Jesus, crucifixion becomes a heroic death, and those who share in it are drawn into Jesus' heroism, even if they have done great wrong. The criminals were led to share the same death as Jesus. And, as we shortly see, one of them becomes the first man to join Jesus in paradise.

So Jesus is not just united with us in suffering, but united with us in condemnation. We who are sinners — motivated by acquisitiveness, jealousy, pride and selfishness — deserve to suffer for our sins. But even if we have done the worst sins of all — sins that require us to be spewed out of the mouth of society as a poison — then in our condemnation and rejection we are united with Jesus. The way of punishment can become the way of salvation. No shame or humiliation will ever bring us lower than Jesus, and because he shared in it, it becomes a gift of divine union. 'He has put down the mighty from their thrones, and exalted those of low degree' (Luke 1:52), and never more truly than when Christ shared not only our suffering and our death, but also our condemnation for wrongdoing.

'He himself bore our sins in his body on the tree, that we might die to sin and live to righteousness' (1 Peter 2:24). Jesus turned everything upside down. He, who had never sinned, suffered a criminal execution that he did not deserve, so that we who are sinners, might share his resurrection that we do not deserve.

Prayer I remember before you, Jesus,
the traitors, torturers,
muggers and rapists of the world.
I remember how you shared their condemnation in the eyes of society,
so as to teach us to love and forgive them.

. . . there they crucified him.

And when they came to the place which is called The Skull, there they crucified him, and the criminals, one on the right and one on the left.

(Luke 23:33)

The 'place which is called The Skull', is called in Latin Calvary, in Hebrew Golgotha, but all three have the same meaning. The place where Jesus was led was a place full of memories of violent killing, human agony and humiliation, even if there were not literally skulls on the ground (as in the picture on p. 95).

We have come to the crucifixion. We no longer look ahead and anticipate it. The worst has arrived. Let us simply watch, and listen. We cannot know how it was, but we can imagine how it might have been.

Let us imagine the thieves fighting and swearing, see a number of soldiers holding their arms still, others catching hold of the other arm and their legs to prevent them fighting. The nails are placed and the hammer lifted. Then there is the screaming. The cross beam is lifted, dragging the body yet more painfully along as more pressure is put on the pinioned hands. Man and beam are lifted — legs held, kicking — set on the bracket of the upright, and a third and final nail twists feet in towards each other and flattens them against the cross. The wood is rough and splintery — not planed, polished and dark-stained like on our crucifixes, but more like the beams you find underneath the floorboards.

The cries and screams of the thieves are to be with us a long time before they die down.

But Jesus does not struggle or scream. He steps forward readily to let himself be stripped. He lays himself on the ground, his shoulders against the beam. A soldier takes his arm; Jesus gives it, then closes his eyes. We hear the clang of the hammer — no other sound. The other arm. A second clang. The lifting of beam and body. The weight now falling, pulling the hands down against the nails, stretching the wounds. The beam fixed, the legs gathered in, the third clang of metal against metal. The crowd of soldiers draws back. We see Jesus on the cross, his arms stretched out, his feet pulled together. We

see his warm living flesh hung up by nails. Sweat trickles from his face, blood from his wounds. He opens his eyes and looks at me.

Prayer I look at you, Jesus, as you are crucified,
and see you look at me,
in silence.

'. . . Father, forgive them.'

And Jesus said, 'Father, forgive them; for they know not what they do.'

(Luke 23:34)

We are not told exactly when Jesus spoke these words, or exactly about whom he spoke them. We often imagine them said as he was nailed to the cross, so that they seemed most immediately to refer to the Roman soldiers responsible for his crucifixion. Or they could have been spoken after the cross was raised, and then it might be a little clearer that they applied to all those with a part in bringing about the crucifixion. That included the chief priests and scribes who had negotiated his arrest and condemnation, the group of men who had arrested him and ill-treated him, and the crowd who had shouted for his death; it included Herod who had failed to release him, Pilate who had finally given the death sentence, and the soldiers who had carried out the crucifixion; it included the disciples who had fled, betrayed or denied him, and each one of us who by our sins have made this redemption necessary.

Luke records three utterances from the cross, of which this is the first. Each one, in Luke, is full of gentleness, compassion and generosity. Today we read 'Father, forgive them; for they know not what they do.' Soon we will come to 'Truly, I say to you, today you will be with me in Paradise,' and 'Father, into thy hands I commit my spirit.'

The gospel of John gives us three different utterances: 'Woman, behold, your son . . . behold, your mother,' 'I thirst' and 'It is finished'. Matthew and Mark record only 'My God, my God, why hast thou forsaken me?' We must be grateful to Luke for giving us these three sentences, without which we would have much less idea of Jesus' mercy and self-giving on the cross.

We are so used to the Christian teaching on forgiveness that often it has washed over our heads, instead of stunning us as something quite extraordinary and revolutionary. Even if we look up Psalm 69 — the very psalm which is recalled when Jesus is given vinegar to drink (see verse 36) — we find a very different attitude there to oppressors. 'Add to them punishment upon punishment;' it says, 'may they have no acquittal from thee. Let them be blotted out of the book of the living' (Psalm 69:27–28).

Prophetic psalm it may be, but Jesus turns upside down its approach to wrongdoers. Those who kill Jesus are not to be punished and 'blotted out' but forgiven, so that they may live. In Jesus' death, meaning is turned on its head, and a new order is begun. Where we thought there was punishment, there is now forgiveness; where we thought there was death, there will shortly be life; where we thought there was shame and condemnation, we will find honour and justification. That is what salvation means.

And so Jesus' words of forgiveness are not just a commendable extra, but express the whole, real, inner meaning of what he is doing in letting himself be crucified. He had said the night before: 'This is my blood of the covenant, which is poured out for many for the forgiveness of sins' (Matthew 26:28). He gave himself over to death so that many people could receive forgiveness; so it was important that as he died he should be forgiving those who killed him.

Again, he stresses the close link between his death and forgiveness when he appears to the disciples after his resurrection. 'Thus it is written, that the Christ should suffer and on the third day rise from the dead, and that repentance and forgiveness of sins should be preached in his name to all nations, beginning from Jerusalem' (Luke 24:46–47).

And Peter makes the link in a very vivid way in his very first speech to the Jerusalem crowd. Those who killed Jesus are offered forgiveness for that sin, a forgiveness that of course comes precisely through his death: ' "God has made him both Lord and Christ, this Jesus whom you crucified." Now when they heard this they were cut to the heart, and said to Peter and the rest of the apostles, "Brethren, what shall we do?" And Peter said to them, "Repent, and be baptized every one of you in the name of Jesus Christ for the forgiveness of your sins" ' (Acts 2:36–38).

Prayer Forgive us our trespasses,
         as we forgive those who trespass against us.

'... Let him save himself.'

And they cast lots to divide his garments. And the people stood by, watching; but the rulers scoffed at him, saying, 'He saved others; let him save himself, if he is the Christ of God, his Chosen One!' The soldiers also mocked him, coming up and offering him vinegar, and saying, 'If you are the King of Jews, save yourself!'

(Luke 23:34–37)

The 'rulers' here are Jewish authorities. Luke has linked them with chief priests earlier, in verse 13, and later on the way to Emmaus: 'our chief priests and rulers delivered him up' (Luke 24:20).

We can remember that the religious trial — before the council — condemned Jesus for claiming to be the Christ and the Son of God; while the condemnation in the political trial — before Pilate — had to be made on the grounds that he called himself a king. The same split of accusations is reflected in the mockery before the cross. The Jewish authorities say 'let him save himself, if he is the Christ of God', while Pilate's soldiers say 'If you are the King of the Jews, save yourself'.

The silent faithfulness of Jesus' followers, who can do nothing to help but be there to watch and share Jesus' sorrows, is contrasted with the mockery of the rulers and soldiers. Almost every detail of this scene is paralleled in Psalm 22, a psalm which Jesus deliberately recalls in his great cry of desolation recorded by Matthew and Mark (not by Luke, whose picture is more of a peaceful, controlled Jesus): 'My God, my God, why hast thou forsaken me?'

One of the passages of the psalm that mirrors most amazingly the passion of Jesus goes like this:

I am poured out like water,
  and all my bones are out of joint . . .
  . . . my tongue cleaves to my jaws;
  thou dost lay me in the dust of death.
Yea, dogs are round about me;
  a company of evildoers encircle me;
  they have pierced my hands and feet —
I can count all my bones —
  they stare and gloat over me;

they divide my garments among them,
    and for my raiment they cast lots.

                    (Psalm 22:14–18)
And so the stretched, hung body of Jesus has all its bones out of joint; his hands and feet are pierced. His tongue cleaves to his jaws, so that (in John) he asks for a drink. (In Luke however the offer of vinegar is treated as an act of mockery, not kindness.) Jesus is to be laid 'in the dust of death'. He is stared at and gloated over, and his garments are divided up and assigned by lot.

Another passage from the psalm speaks more vividly about mockery:
But I am a worm, and no man;
    scorned by men, and despised by the people.
All who see me mock at me,
    they make mouths at me, they wag their heads;
'He committed his cause to the LORD; let him deliver him,
    let him rescue him, for he delights in him!'
                    (Psalm 22:6–8)
That echoes the account we are given in Luke: they scoffed 'let him save himself, if he is the Christ of God'; they mocked 'If you are the King of the Jews, save yourself'.

And Jesus, who wanted so much that people should recognize who he was and how he could help them, had to hold back from giving them the proof they tauntingly asked for. What a temptation — to end his agony, and win their belief, in the same act of self-rescue! How painful it must have been to hear these words, and do nothing.

Prayer They have pierced your hands and feet, Jesus.
        They make mouths at you, they wag their heads.
        I do believe in you, though you do not save yourself.

'... the King of the Jews.'

There was also an inscription over him, in letters of Greek and Latin and Hebrew, 'This is the King of the Jews.'

(Luke 23:38)

We are all familiar with seeing INRI written over crucifixes (we can see it in the picture on p. 95), and some of us may know that the letters stand for the Latin version of 'Jesus of Nazareth, King of the Jews'. Each of the four gospels record this notice, though they have slight differences in phrasing. John alone has the full INRI text, 'Jesus of Nazareth, the King of the Jews'.

But did Jesus claim to be the King of the Jews? We have already seen that this title was the one used by the chief priests to persuade Pilate to put Jesus to death, when the titles *they* seemed more offended by were 'the Christ', and 'the Son of God'. But the Messiah was foretold as a king, so to that extent Jesus was indeed King of the Jews.

These claims for Jesus are all made earlier in Luke's gospel, in situations of decisive importance. Peter's profession of faith, that led into the witnessing of the transfiguration, had been that Jesus was 'the Christ of God' (Luke 9:20). And the crowd, as they joyfully welcomed Jesus' entry into Jerusalem, had cried out 'Blessed is the King who comes in the name of the Lord!' (Luke 19:38).

And yet, it could be highly misleading to think of Jesus as a king, especially as a king of the Jews, which suggested a political revolutionary. That is why Jesus could neither deny this title nor affirm it without qualification, in his famous words before Pilate recorded in John's gospel: 'My kingship is not of this world . . . You say that I am king. For this I was born, and for this I have come into the world, to bear witness to the truth' (John 18:36–37).

If Jesus is a king, he is king of heaven, sharing in God's kingship. What Jesus comes to preach is the kingdom of God. We recall this every time we say the 'Our Father': 'Thy kingdom come . . . ' And then, with an almost imperceptible movement, the New Testament slips, here and there, from calling God the king, to calling Christ the king, so that almost without realizing it we find we have reached the point of recognizing Christ as divine.

And so, in 1 Timothy, it is God who is spoken of triumphantly as the 'only Sovereign, the King of kings and Lord of lords, who alone has immortality

86

and dwells in unapproachable light . . . ' (1 Timothy 6:15–16). But in the book of Revelation we find that this title is given to the Lamb, that is, to the sacrificed Jesus: the Lamb is 'Lord of lords and King of kings' (Revelation 17:14).

What all this means for us is that when we turn to Jesus and call him *our* King, we are recognizing him as our God. We think of him as the King who is to come, in great glory and might and judgment, and pray, like the penitent thief we will be considering tomorrow, that Jesus will remember us when he comes into his kingdom. Or we may cast that kingly image back in time, and think of Jesus as king already on the cross. Perhaps we have seen crucifixes that show Jesus with a crown on his head, as it were enthroned on a cross, with arms stretched wide in kingly glory. These crucifixes show the sort of king we want — a king who gives his life — and the sort of kingdom we want — a kingdom where truth and justice are valued more than comfort and life itself.

A man dying on a cross is a strange sort of King to serve, and a strange sort of God to worship. If we really took in all the implications of this upside-down kingdom of the crucified Christ we would live our lives completely differently, and find our habitual values constantly overthrown. We would find ourselves making choices against security, against prudence, against money, against social acceptability, as we pledge our lives in service to the man who became the lowest of the low. It is that dying man on a cross who will be, who already in a sense is, the King of kings.

Prayer Remember me, Jesus, when you come into your kingdom.

'. . . Today you will be with me in Paradise.'

One of the criminals who were hanged railed at him, saying, 'Are you not the Christ? Save yourself and us!' But the other rebuked him, saying, 'Do you not fear God, since you are under the same sentence of condemnation? And we indeed justly; for we are receiving the due reward of our deeds; but this man has done nothing wrong.' And he said, 'Jesus, remember me when you come into your kingdom.' And he said to him, 'Truly, I say to you, today you will be with me in Paradise.'

(Luke 23:39–43)

Today is Palm Sunday, which sometimes now is called Passion Sunday, the very day when we celebrate Jesus' entry into Jerusalem as 'the King who comes in the name of the Lord', and today, too, we read the text in which the repentant thief recognizes the kingdom of Christ. So the theme of Christ the king, that we looked at yesterday, continues on this first day of Holy Week.

This story of Jesus' mercy to the thief is not even hinted at in any other gospel. Indeed in Matthew and Mark both the criminals join in the reproaches of the crowd. Luke's first criminal is clearly doing just that when he says, 'Are you not the Christ? Save yourself and us!', picking up so closely the taunts of the Jewish authorities in verse 35. And so this criminal joins the side of those who have crucified Jesus, while the second criminal freely aligns himself with Jesus in accepting the fate of crucifixion.

The penitence of this criminal shows itself in two ways: firstly, in acknowledging that he is a sinner, who has deserved punishment by the way he has lived up till now; secondly, in showing faith in Jesus, and faith of a remarkable sort. His faith goes beyond the grave, for he realizes that Jesus will not suddenly leap from the cross and so show that he is the Christ of God. Jesus will indeed come into his kingdom, but he will first suffer the full effects of crucifixion. This Christ, this King, will die before his kingdom comes.

And this belief was something not even Jesus' closest disciples, the twelve, could take in, not even when Jesus warned them of it repeatedly. We saw that (on p. 39 above) when Jesus prophesied his passion and the disciples 'did not understand'. We saw it again when one of the disciples thought he should resist the arrest with violence, and cut off the ear of a slave (see p. 48). But the thief can accept that even though Jesus is on the next cross to him, panting out his last breaths, even though he seems utterly defeated and destroyed, yet he will come into his kingdom. And he is brave enough to speak out his faith amid the general taunts.

'Today you will be with me in Paradise.' No matter what we have done, how much we have stolen, how many deaths we have been responsible for (in the modern world where millions starve there is blood on the hands of all of us) . . . no matter even if we come to the hour of our death and we have done nothing and it is now too late to remedy any of the suffering we have caused . . . no matter how great our sin, we can be forgiven, if we truly acknowledge it, in faith.

Just as Jesus offended the chief priests and elders by telling them 'the tax collectors and the harlots go into the kingdom of God before you' (Matthew 21:31), so here again he promises the first place in Paradise to one of the worst sinners, and for the same reason, because he repented and believed (see Matthew 21:32).

And, since he really did believe, what joy the thief must have felt at Jesus' words. How he must have longed to die, to be taken up with Jesus to share his reward, just as he had shared Jesus' fate. It is much easier to endure pain, when we know it will soon end, and after it ends there will be an indescribable joy. That is the hope that sustains a woman through labour, when she suffers greatly but hopes greatly, and when her child is born she has such joy as cannot be measured because it is the joy of a new love, and love cannot be measured. So too the thief, and so too Jesus, could look ahead, and endure the agony of the cross (and no greater torture can be imagined than that), in the faith that within a few hours they would enter Paradise, and enter it together. How typical of Jesus to choose as his first companion in Paradise a disgraced criminal. How like the rest of Jesus' ministry. And how unlike our own values.

Prayer May I be with you, one day, in Paradise.

. . . the curtain of the temple was torn.

It was now about the sixth hour, and there was darkness over the whole land until the ninth hour, while the sun's light failed; and the curtain of the temple was torn in two.

(Luke 23:44–45)

The sixth hour is noon, and the ninth hour three p.m. Churches that celebrate their Good Friday liturgy at three o'clock do so to mark the approximate time of Jesus' death. But there is confusion over these timings. Mark has Jesus crucified at the third hour, i.e. nine a.m. (Mark 15:25), allowing very little time for the trial, scourging and mockery beforehand, while John tells us it was already midday before the trial with Pilate was over (John 19:14). In general we tend to compromise and think of Jesus on the cross, as Luke suggests, for about three hours, or slightly more, from midday till just after three p.m.

It really is very hard to imagine the torture of being alive on a cross for three hours, with the whole body weight dragging against the nails, with the constriction on breathing that comes from being held up by the arms, and with every tiny movement causing new, intense pain.

That the Son of God should suffer this is so unthinkable that we are not surprised when Luke tells us that not only Jesus' followers stand by and mourn, but nature itself broke its rhythm, as it were to close its eyes and grieve. The sun's light failed and there was darkness at noon.

The Jews of the time would have understood this darkness as a fulfilment of prophecy. Peter, in his first speech at Pentecost, quotes from the prophet Joel:

> the sun shall be turned into darkness
> and the moon into blood,
> before the day of the Lord comes,
> the great and manifest day.

(Acts 2:20)

90

Another prophecy, from Amos, actually talks of darkness at noon:
'And on that day,' says the Lord GOD,
  'I will make the sun go down at noon,
  and darken the earth in broad daylight.
I will turn your feasts into mourning,
  and all your songs into lamentation.'
(Amos 8:9–10)
So the darkness is a sign of mourning, and a sign of the day of the Lord. It is also a sign of evil, as Jesus himself had expressed it on the Mount of Olives: 'This is your hour, and the power of darkness.'

The second sign reported by Luke is the tearing of the curtain in the temple. Like the darkness it is disturbing and dramatic. Like the darkness, it seems to say 'after this, the world will never be the same again'. But this seeming act of destruction — a rending apart — is also a sign of the new order.

From now on the old covenant — the old rule of Jewish law — is over. The curtain is torn down the middle — 'from top to bottom' in Matthew and Mark — and the inner holy of holies, the intimate secrets of God himself, are laid open to humanity. Up till now only the high priest had been allowed to enter the holy of holies, protected by this curtain, and then only on the Day of Atonement. But the day of Jesus' crucifixion is the new Day of Atonement, when he tears open the barriers between us and God, and the world is reconciled to its maker.

'Therefore, brethren, since we have confidence to enter the sanctuary by the blood of Jesus, by the new and living way which he opened for us through the curtain, that is, through his flesh, and since we have a great priest over the house of God, let us draw near with a true heart in full assurance of faith, with our hearts sprinkled clean from an evil conscience and our bodies washed with pure water' (Hebrews 10:19–22).

How powerfully this passage from Hebrews takes up the theme of the tearing of the curtain. Our bodies are washed in clean water, and our sins forgiven. We approach the sanctuary, now veiled not by the old curtain but by the curtain of Christ, the new high priest, the great priest. We approach God with confidence, with full assurance, with a true heart. Christ's body is broken, his blood spilled, and we pass through the midst of his body, into the sanctuary, into the presence of God.

Prayer Grant me the confidence, Jesus,
        to pass through the torn curtain of your flesh,
        into the presence of God.

'. . . into thy hands I commit my spirit.'

Then Jesus, crying with a loud voice, said, 'Father, into thy hands I commit my spirit!' And having said this he breathed his last.
(Luke 23:46)

On this Tuesday of Holy Week, after six weeks preparation, we finally reach the death, the pivot point of redemption history. We reach the point of climax, and the point of release, the moment when Jesus' self-offering was consummated, and his work on earth completed. It is good to meditate on this moment in the very week in which the Church remembers the death of Jesus.

First Jesus cries out with a loud voice. (It is clearer in the Greek that 'Father, into thy hands . . .' was not the loud cry, but came after it.) Luke does not tell us what this cry was — it could be just an inarticulate shout — but Matthew and Mark both record Jesus crying out with a loud voice at this moment: 'Eli, Eli, lama sabachthani?' which means 'My God, my God, why hast thou forsaken me?' Once one has got one's tongue round the syllables, the four words of Hebrew form themselves more easily into an anguished shout than the English translation.

'Into thy hands I commit my spirit' is a quotation from a psalm (Psalm 31:5). The psalm continues with a passage of great anguish: 'I have passed out of mind like one who is dead; I have become like a broken vessel' (verse 12). Jesus' prayer on the cross springs from the heart of his deep Jewish faith, in which cries for help and prayers of trust are constantly intertwined.

'Father, into thy hands I commit my spirit' is such a perfect prayer, such a beautiful and simple expression of generous and trusting love, that we too should make the prayer our own as Jesus did. One way to use it is in bed at night as we give ourselves into sleep in the Lord's hands. If we can live with some awareness of this giving over of our spirit into the safety of God's hands, then we will truly be letting Christ live in us.

And when Jesus had said those words, he died. Literally the Greek is telling us that he breathed out his spirit (it is significantly an unusual word

92

that is used for his death), so that his dying really was a committal of his spirit into God's hands.

At Jesus' death we may feel a great relief, a great stillness, as his agony is over, his restless pain released.

But we may also feel a great and terrible emptiness. It is a greater emptiness than when anyone else dies, because it is the death not just of the meaning of *my* life (as when someone very dear to me dies) but of the Meaning of Life itself. Jesus came in time, in history, and was known by those around him, and yet came for all time, for all history, and is known by all of us. He belongs to us all as no one else does. He is needed by us all as no one else is. And when he dies, it is not just a hole in our life, but emptiness itself, meaninglessness itself, destruction itself. Or it would be, if we did not know that this emptiness, meaninglessness and destruction will last for three days only. Were there no Jesus, were there never more to be any Jesus, then what would be the point of living? How would there be hope that we could become what God made us to be?

Jesus' death leaves a great stillness, a great silence. Something has gone greater than we could ever find words to express. He fought with evil spirits and routed them . . . he stilled the winds and the waves with a word . . . he healed the sick and raised the dead . . . he spoke to sinners and changed their lives . . . he called disciples and they left all and followed him . . . he debated with scribes and left them confused and defeated . . .

Now he himself lies dead, contorted on the cross, there is nothing to say, and no one left to say it to. We hear, perhaps, the last moanings and gaspings of the two criminals, the chatter and quips of the soldiers for whom this is just an ordinary day's work, and the hysterical weeping of Mary Magdalene. Beyond that lies a great and empty silence.

Prayer   Father, into thy hands I commit my spirit.
May your dying, Jesus,
enter into my living.

... they saw what had taken place.

Now when the centurion saw what had taken place, he praised God, and said, 'Certainly this man was innocent!' And all the multitudes who assembled to see the sight, when they saw what had taken place, returned home beating their breasts. And all his acquaintances and the women who had followed him from Galilee stood at a distance and saw these things.

(Luke 23:47–49)

Those gathered around the cross see Jesus die. The centurion 'saw what had taken place', the multitudes were there 'to see the sight', and those who knew Jesus 'saw these things'. The people do very little, and they say very little, but they are present and they watch. They see.

Following Jesus (like 'the women who had followed him') may not involve us in *doing* anything very much; it may just mean that we are present to him and we see him. That is why one of the purest forms of prayer is sometimes called the prayer of 'simple regard', which means the prayer of just looking. We are often so caught up in being busy that we find it hard to make time to stop doing things so that we can just see.

What is this life if, full of care,

We have no time to stand and stare?

Today we are invited to stand and stare, not at beautiful green fields and woods, but at the dead Jesus.

The extraordinary fact about the people round the cross, who abandon all their duties for the day simply to be with Jesus, looking at him, is that they are changed by the experience. Just seeing, doing nothing, turns out to be for them a revolutionary experience, so that afterwards they see things differently and, no doubt, will act differently. They have not wasted their time in doing nothing, but they have allowed themselves to be changed.

Before the death of Jesus we were told how everyone was mocking and taunting him. Now, his agony over, a change has come over the scene. The centurion does not cry 'Now you can never be a king, now you are dead!' but he praises God, saying 'Certainly this man was innocent'. And the multitudes beat their breasts in repentance. Judgments are altered, people

see things in a different light, and they feel both sorrow for their own sinfulness and praise for God's goodness.

That is how the scene struck those who were present, and we too want to share in that response. We want to see the dying of Jesus with eyes opened to its transforming power, so that we too can be changed, be sorry for our sins, and give praise to God.

Prayer Looking at you on the cross, Jesus,
       I ask forgiveness for my sins,
       and I praise God.

HOLY THURSDAY (OR MAUNDY THURSDAY)

... asked for the body.

Now there was a man named Joseph from the Jewish town of Arimathea. He was a member of the council, a good and righteous man, who had not consented to their purpose and deed, and he was looking for the kingdom of God. This man went to Pilate and asked for the body of Jesus.

(Luke 23:50–52)

We know very little about Joseph of Arimathea. He had his own stone-hewn tomb, and Matthew's gospel describes him explicitly as rich. He was also a member of the council, which so shortly before had found Jesus guilty. He had not consented to the general verdict, but we are not told that he openly fought it. John tells us that he was a disciple, but in secret for fear of the Jews. Perhaps he had tried to hold back the council in a moderate way, without disclosing that he actually was a believer, much as Nicodemus, another secret disciple from the Jewish authorities, had done (John 7:51). The names of Nicodemus and Joseph of Arimathea are linked in John's gospel when they lay out the body of Jesus, but in the synoptic gospels Joseph alone is mentioned.

We saw yesterday how Jesus' death affected the spectators, and made them repent. We can imagine that Joseph may have felt very badly at not having declared his allegiance to Jesus openly, and at having allowed the condemnation to go through while still fearfully hiding what he really believed.

Joseph has followed through the events of the day with, no doubt, considerable stress. First thing in the morning had been the emergency meeting of the council, at which he had been present. Then 'the whole company of them' had accompanied Jesus to Pilate's palace. When he had lived through those battles, and seen the fateful outcome, he had followed Jesus out to Calvary, stayed with him through his three hours (or more) of crucifixion, and finally seen him die. Now, undoubtedly moved by the experience and possible ashamed of his secrecy up till now, he goes back into Jerusalem to seek an immediate audience with Pilate and ask for the body. It was, as Mark admits, an act of courage when the rest of the Jewish council

96

were congratulating themselves on their success: he 'took courage and went to Pilate' (Mark 15:43).

Joseph asks for the body of Jesus, and it is given him. On this very day, Holy Thursday, we commemorate the moment when Jesus gave his body to all of us. 'This is my body which is given for you' (Luke 22:19). When the body of Jesus is handed out to us so easily in church we forget that to ask for it is an act of allegiance, that can sometimes become an act of courage.

The body Joseph asked for was a dead body. Yet it meant so much to him. The hands that had healed the sick, now wounded and stiff . . . the feet that had travelled from town to town, now with holes in them . . . the eyes that had looked at people, and looked through into their hearts . . . the mouth that had preached . . . the face that had lit up with the love of God . . . the figure that people had flocked to see. The body Joseph asked for was a sad remnant of a man he loved.

How dear and precious that lifeless body — greying, stiffening, losing its warmth. Even more dear and precious is the body that Jesus gives all of us on this day in his eucharist — the risen body, not dead and useless, but risen and life-giving. We stretch out our hands for Jesus, and he gives us himself. 'This is my body which is given for you.' Now we have watched with him through his passion we understand more than ever before what it means for him to give us his body. Now we can bring also to the eucharist the memory of Joseph of Arimathea, and we hope to ask for the body of Jesus with no less love than he felt; with no less awareness of the preciousness of what we ask for; with no less shame for the cowardice of our half-hearted and half-hidden commitment to Jesus; and with no less readiness, now, to waste no time in doing the right and needed thing.

Joseph of Arimathea was 'a good and righteous man' who was 'looking for the kingdom of God'. He did not stop looking for it because every hope of it now seemed smashed. On the contrary, he now showed a courage and a decisiveness, through the death of Jesus, that he seemed not to have found his way to before. Sometimes greater courage can come through greater pain.

Prayer As I ask for your body, Jesus,
I ask also for your forgiveness.

. . . he took it down.

Then he took it down and wrapped it in a linen shroud, and laid him in a rock-hewn tomb, where no one had ever yet been laid.

(Luke 23:53)

'. . . we call this Friday good', said T. S. Eliot. We like to think that ordinary life is normal and good, while death is absurd and bad, but today we see things differently.

> The dripping blood our only drink,
> The bloody flesh our only food:
> In spite of which we like to think
> That we are sound, substantial flesh and blood —
> Again, in spite of that, we call this Friday good.
>
> *(East Coker)*

Today we recognize the death of Christ as something good, and we remember that we have entered into that death in our baptism. We have died, and our life is hid with Christ in God (see Colossians 3:3).

Joseph of Arimathea took down the body of Jesus. He probably put a ladder to the cross, wrenched out the nails from the hands with a pair of pincers, and, with the help of others, let the body be lowered forward into his arms.

'And if a man has committed a crime punishable by death and he is put to death, and you hang him on a tree, his body shall not remain all night upon the tree, but you shall bury him the same day, for a hanged man is accursed by God' (Deuteronomy 21:22–23).

So Christ became 'a curse for us' (Galatians 3:13), for he 'bore our sins in his body on the tree' (1 Peter 2:24). But Joseph did not take his body down as something accursed by God, but as something holy and precious.

He carried down the heavy weight of Jesus' dead body and wrapped it in a linen shroud. Corpses are wrapped up, partly to spare our sight, and partly because they are precious. Joseph wrapped up the body of Jesus, as we might wrap a baby in a shawl, with tenderness. He laid him in a new tomb, where no one had ever yet been laid, as we might take a tired child in our arms, and tuck it warmly and safely into a newly-made bed. The body of Jesus was

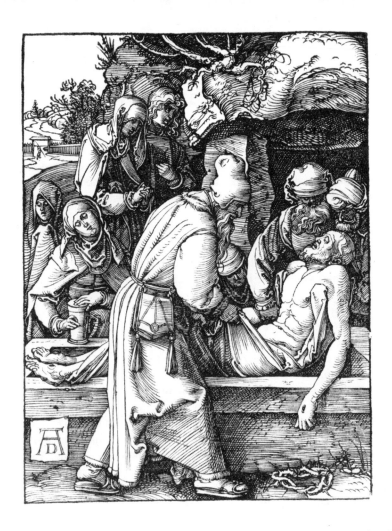

hidden from our sight, in a clean shroud, in a new tomb, and it was preciously hidden. And Christ was hid in God.

Prayer Precious, dearly loved Jesus,
you hide us with you in God,
in this week that we call holy,
on this Friday that we call good.

... on the sabbath they rested.

It was the day of Preparation, and the sabbath was beginning. The women who had come with him from Galilee followed, and saw the tomb, and how his body was laid; then they returned, and prepared spices and ointments. On the sabbath they rested according to the commandment.

(Luke 23:54–56)

The women saw Jesus' body laid in the tomb. They witnessed with their own eyes how and where the corpse was left. They could not afterwards say 'Perhaps we went to the wrong tomb . . . Perhaps they forgot to put the body in before they closed it . . . '

They saw Jesus' body in the tomb, and as they went back for the sabbath rest, they carried that picture printed on their minds, just as, some people believe, the picture of Jesus' body was soon to be printed on the shroud that wrapped him.

The women must have longed for more time, to anoint the body before the sabbath. But in a beautiful symbolism, Jesus' body had already been anointed for its burial, at the supper at Bethany, when a woman had poured a flask of pure nard over his head. Jesus had said: 'She has done a beautiful thing to me . . . she has anointed my body beforehand for burying. And truly, I say to you, wherever the gospel is preached in the whole world, what she has done will be told in memory of her' (Mark 14:6–9).

The fragrant anointing that was lacking now, had been lovingly and extravagantly performed then. The women need not have worried that they had no time for it, and never, now, would have time for it, for when they came back with their prepared spices and ointments, it would be too late. The Christ, the 'anointed one', had already received his anointing. It had been an anointing for burial, and now he has been both anointed and buried.

With Jesus dead and buried, we can let our memories run back to those first days of Lent, when we meditated on Peter's profession of faith. No wonder then that Jesus had deliberately linked his role as the Christ, the 'anointed one', with his death: 'And Peter answered, "The Christ of God." But he charged and commanded them to tell this to no one, saying, "The Son of man must suffer many things, and be rejected by the elders and chief priests and scribes, and be killed, and on the third day be raised" ' (Luke 9:20–22).

Now that we have lived through that story with Jesus (all but the raising) we understand more deeply that this 'anointed one' was anointed for death.

Jesus is dead. He is buried. The sabbath rest has fallen on the world. The women must wait, we must wait, Jesus must wait. 'As Jonah was three days and three nights in the belly of the whale, so will the Son of man be three days and three nights in the heart of the earth' (Matthew 12:40).

Women know a lot about waiting. They wait most fruitfully of all when they are expecting a baby. The child is hidden from sight, closed up in the womb, but when the months are fulfilled we see how much has developed during the time of waiting. As a baby grows in the darkness of the womb, as Jonah lay in the belly of the whale, so the body of Jesus waits in the closed, dark tomb.

The seventh day, the sabbath day, is the day when the Jews shared in the great rest of God. 'So God blessed the seventh day and hallowed it, because on it God rested from all his work which he had done in creation' (Genesis 2:3). There was no labour like Jesus' passion, and no rest more profound than the stillness that followed it.

But the first day — tomorrow's day — is the day of explosive creativity, the day when God created the heavens and the earth, the day when God said, 'Let there be light'. As we wait, sharing in God's rest, sharing in Jesus' death, seeing the buried body lie still in the darkened, closed tomb, what we are waiting for is the new creation.

Prayer I rest, with you Jesus, in the tomb.
 I wait, with you Jesus, for the new creation.

'. . . He is not here, but has risen.'

But on the first day of the week, at early dawn, they went to the tomb, taking the spices which they had prepared. And they found the stone rolled away from the tomb, but when they went in they did not find the body of the Lord Jesus. While they were perplexed about this, behold, two men stood by them in dazzling apparel; and as they were frightened and bowed their faces to the ground, the men said to them, 'Why do you seek the living among the dead? He is not here, but has risen. Remember how he told you, while he was still in Galilee, that the Son of man must be delivered into the hands of sinful men, and be crucified, and on the third day rise.' And they remembered his words, and returning from the tomb they told all this to the eleven and to all the rest. Now it was Mary Magdalene and Joanna and Mary the mother of James and the other women with them who told this to the apostles; but these words seemed to them an idle tale, and they did not believe them. But Peter rose and ran to the tomb; stooping and looking in, he saw the linen cloths by themselves; and he went home wondering at what had happened.

(Luke 24:1–12)

This first Easter story of Luke's does not record the actual event of resurrection. Luke does not describe the great burst of exploding light that tore open the gates of hell and brought Jesus triumphantly out of the tomb. Rather, he tells us of what the women saw — first, a rolled-away stone, then, an empty tomb, then, two men in shining clothes. They are not straightaway triumphant and joyful, but first perplexed, and soon so frightened they fall on their faces. It takes time for them to get used to the idea that Jesus is risen. Dead bodies simply do not get up and walk. The unknown is alarming; the seeds of joy and relief take time to grow.

We, perhaps, have switched into resurrection-gear more smoothly. We knew it was coming, so are not frightened by the unexpected. We have maybe already been to church and joined in a joyous, light-filled, flower-decked, music-trumpeting liturgy. It is easier for us.

Of course we are right to celebrate, and to celebrate unreservedly. The resurrection of Jesus gives the first real justification in human history for uninhibited joy: there is no disaster that is not redeemed by Easter. Pain . . . death . . . sin . . . failure . . . hell . . . all are overcome. But it is helpful also if we can let ourselves remember the fearful, puzzling side of Easter as well; then we can recognize the fear and puzzlement we sometimes feel ourselves about the resurrection, and learn to take it in our stride. The most stupendously marvellous things about God make us afraid, but we lift ourselves off our faces and take courage to rejoice.

It is like the transfiguration, all over again, but this time the joy has no shadow and the glory is for ever. Many details of the transfiguration story can now be recognized as pointing forward to the resurrection story.

'And behold, two men talked with him' (Luke 9:30) and 'behold, two men stood by them' (Luke 24:4). The first time they are identified as Moses and Elijah, the second time they are usually thought of as angels, but the parallelism in the vivid phrase 'behold, two men' is striking; it is to occur again at that other decisive moment of glory, the ascension: 'behold, two men stood by them in white robes' (Acts 1:10).

We may recall how Jesus' clothes at the transfiguration were said to be 'dazzling white' (literally, to 'flash forth like lightning'), and here in the Easter story the clothes of the two men are described as 'dazzling', or 'flashing' like lightning. The angels remind the women of the prophecy Jesus had made of his death and resurrection — the very prophecy that had been made just before, and just after, the transfiguration itself (Luke 9:22, 44).

The transfiguration seems to have happened at first dawn, when the disciples were heavy with sleep, but woke to see Christ's glory. So too, the resurrection occurs at early dawn, and the first witnesses are those who are first up. Jesus, our light, rises like the sun, but outshines it for brightness.

We could draw a parallel, also, between the three male disciples named at the Mount of transfiguration, and the three female disciples named at the empty tomb. Peter, James and John are witnesses to the transfiguration; Mary Magdalene, Joanna and Mary the mother of James are the first to hear the news that Jesus has risen.

So when we read that the women 'were frightened and bowed their faces to the ground', we remember that we have met this fear before. On the Mount of transfiguration the disciples 'were afraid' (Luke 9:34), and 'fell on their faces' (Matthew 17:6). Let us too not be afraid *to be afraid*, because the glory of God, that now enters fully into his Son Jesus, is so great and dazzling, as it breaks forth like lightning before us, that we want to fall and worship.

Prayer I worship you, risen Lord,
in fear and joy.

The breaking of the bread.

Prayer Be with us, Jesus,
when we journey, when we rest,
when we break bread, when we share thoughts,
when we doubt, when we believe,
today and always. Amen.